THE AMAZING ASH BARTY

Published in 2022 by Welbeck Publishing Pty Ltd,
part of Welbeck Publishing Group,

Offices in:
London - 20 Mortimer Street, London W1T 3JW
Sydney - 205 Commonwealth Street, Surry Hills 2010

www.welbeckpublishing.com

Design by Julie Hally

ISBN: 9781922853004

Welbeck acknowledges the Traditional Owners and Custodians of this land and gives respect to the Elders – past and present – and through them to all Australian Aboriginal and Torres Strait Islander people.

Printed and bound in Australia by McPherson's Printing Group

10 9 8 7 6 5 4 3 2 1

A catalogue record for this book is available from the National Library of Australia

Statistics and records correct as of August 2022

The paper in this book is FSC® certified. FSC® promotes environmentally responsible, socially beneficial and economically viable management of the world's forests.

THE AMAZING ASH BARTY

James Knight

Illustrated by

Jules Faber

WELBECK

CONTENTS

CHAPTER ONE

IT'S YOUR PARTY

Imagine what it would feel like to be one of the world's greatest tennis players...

It's Saturday, January 29th 2022. It's a mild evening in Melbourne. On the grassy banks of the Yarra River families are making the most of the fading light. A frisbee flies high, cutting the air that is layered with the smell of barbeques. Nearby, a runner surges along the track, while a tram ring-dings its farewell from a stop on St Kilda Road.

What a beautiful evening!

But it is also one filled with nerves...

Just imagine that you, yes ***YOU***, are the world's number one ranked women's tennis player, entering Rod Laver Arena at Melbourne Park, for the Women's Singles Final at the Australian Open.

A crowd of about 12,000 people tower in tiers above you, and the arena's lights sparkle like diamonds. Beyond them, the stars will soon come out.

But YOU are the star that everyone has come to see!

The crowd cheers at every step you take! Banners and flags are waved!

And let's not forget the record-breaking **3.5 million other people** (give or take a few 100,000!) who are watching on televisions around Australia.

Do you know what this means? You are not only carrying a bag of racquets onto the arena, but you are also lugging the weight of a whole nation's hopes...

The last Australian woman to win the Australian Open was Chris O'Neill way back in 1978. Do some maths – **2022-1978 = 44 years** – that is a **LONG** time ago! (The internet wasn't around back then, and it was only nine years after American astronauts Neil Armstrong and Buzz Aldrin became the first people to walk on the moon!)

Now, on this windless evening at *Rod Laver Arena*, another American stands between you and rare air. She is Danielle Collins, a powerful player whose determination is like the universe – it's too big to measure.

Danielle is fired up to beat you!

But you have the first victory of the evening. You win the toss and elect to serve.

Take a deep breath.

And then another. Are you ready to do this?

Don't think of the pressure. You can only do your best, and your reputation won't be defined by whether you win or lose.

Above all, this is a moment for you to embrace. You are here to have fun. So, good luck.

Now... get to it.

THWACK, thwack!

At 7.45pm, the first point of the match is over. You serve down the centre service-line, and Danielle Collins stretches to play a backhand return but hits the ball into the net. The crowd roars.

"The simplest of points, the loudest of ovations," says a commentator.

15–love to you.

You follow up with some booming serves. 160, 170, 180 kilometres an hour. Blink and you miss them. Such power. Such precision.

The match is enthralling.

Backhand! Forehand!

Backhand! Forehand!

Lob! Smash! Volley!

Yellow flashes.

Split seconds.

Muscles straining.

Hearts pounding.

Lungs burning.

On and on it goes until you gain the upper hand and **win the first set.**

6-3 to you.

Amid your fans, there is a sea of people dressed in bright yellow t-shirts with red emblems. They look like living jars of Vegemite, but you look more closely and see **your name** is emblazoned across their chests.

Elsewhere in a box for special guests, Rod Laver smiles. **Australia's greatest ever tennis player knows how good you are!**

But forget about the spectators. Right now, you must concentrate. Every point must be fought for. Danielle Collins knows that too, and she reaches deep inside herself to find the strength that is needed to push you into a corner.

She breaks your serve. Not once, but twice, and suddenly the scoreboard says the unthinkable.

You are trailing 5-1 in the second set.

How did that happen?

Well, that's the beauty of sport. Nothing is assured until the contest is over. And yes, right now, you know the contest is far from over.

Concentrate! **Come on,**

Be the best that you can be in every single moment. It's up to you.

Forehand winner down the line! **BANG!**

Another forehand. **BELTER!**

Then an ace.

A sizzling return.

Another forehand...

Numbers on the scoreboard flick and tick...

And listen to the crowd! The arena has turned into a cauldron with emotions that simmer and bubble, and chatter that swirls from row to row, aisle to aisle.

But you remain calm for point after point, game after game. You swivel, you spin, you sprint across the court, sweat drips from your brow, and the crowd gasps and sighs and gasps again.

Until...

Until...

Until...

"**Six games all.**" says the chair umpire.

What a fightback. You have grabbed hold of momentum and torn it away from Danielle Collins.

Now, for the tie-breaker. You may as well call it a tightrope that is suspended high above the arena's retractable roof. One wrong move and...

Forget that thought. Just concentrate. You know the story: the first player to win seven points (and be two or more ahead of their opponent) wins the set.

And if YOU win this set…
YOU WIN the

The crowd senses the occasion. 1978 champion, Chris O'Neill, is watching. So too are movie star Russell Crowe, and gold medal winning Olympic legends Cathy Freeman and Ian Thorpe. They all know that success is built on years of hard work.

And then there are the people who are so very close to home for you: mum, dad, and your two sisters. They are all part of your journey. And they all know what this evening means to you.

The next few minutes happen in a blur.

1–0

2–0

3–0

4–0

Danielle Collins finally wins a point:

4–1

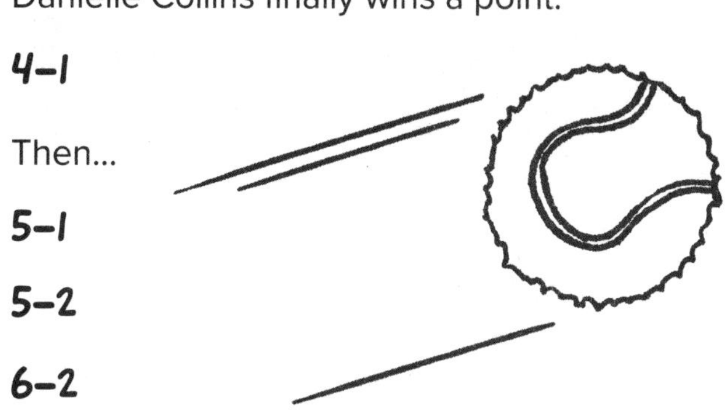

Then…

5–1

5–2

6–2

Is this really happening?

A dream sitting on the edge of reality. You are so close, ***so close***.

Keep calm, control those nerves.

Remember:

The contest is

Danielle Collins stands at the other end of the court. You wait, leaning forward, shoulders swaying from side to side.

Danielle tosses the ball high, then her racquet swings and connects sweetly.

See it, hear it, ***feel it***.

The ball is in play. Watch it, ***watch it!***

You move to your left. Short, sharp, precise.

A backhand.

Another one.

And another.

On the fifth stroke, Danielle Collins advances and sends the ball deep into your court. You run from left to right behind your baseline. You draw your racquet back.

By now, the rally has been going about ten seconds.

(That's time enough for Usain Bolt to sizzle over 100 metres. Time enough for the quickest of minds and slickest of fingers to solve a Rubik's cube.)

But right now, as you play a forehand cross-court, it seems as though time is almost standing still.

Almost...

You watch the ball as it springs off your strings and travels over the net and past your opponent. At this very moment, you may be one of only two players on the court, ***but you are not alone***.

In the arena and across Australia there are millions of eyes seeing what you see, and millions of breaths being held.

This is the moment for us all.

YOU have brought us all together.

An instant later, the ball lands, the crowd erupts! And you yell!

You, yes ***YOU*** have done it.

YOU are Ash Barty.

And this is your party.

CHAPTER TWO

THE GIRL FROM IPSWICH

Okay, before we go any further, it's important to tell you about the word **BELIEF**.

Yes, it's just one single, small word, but when it comes to sport it roars off the page and charges into the heart and mind!

From handball courts in the middle of the school playground to football fields in the middle of the suburbs to cricket pitches in the middle of 100,000-seat stadiums, belief never needs a ticket to be part of the action.

Here's just one example: the annual three-game State of Origin rugby league series between the New South Wales *Blues* and the Queensland *Maroons*. This battle of the border gives rise to all sorts of emotions.

Forget the fireworks, just watch and listen to the crowd!

Tears and laughter, cheers and chants, boos, fists shaking, feet stomping, fingers pointing, and arms flying so wildly above heads that they look as though they're streamers in a cyclone.

Yep, welcome to State of Origin!

In 1995 (long enough ago for your teachers to be young!) the *Blues* were expected to thrash the *Maroons*. In fact, only dreamers gave Queensland a chance of winning. **BUT** in Game One at the Sydney Football Stadium, the *Maroons* stunned all their critics when they led 2-0 at halftime.

Surely, they couldn't win, could they?

Well, one person certainly thought they could.

As the *Maroons* walked out of their dressing room and down the tunnel towards the field to begin the second half, the veteran player Billy Moore yelled:

"Queenslander!
Queenslander!
Queenslander!"

The words sent shivers down the spines of everyone who heard them, and the force of Billy's belief was

SO POWERFUL

that his teammates were jolted with an intensity that helped achieve the unachievable.

They won the game and went on to make a clean sweep of the series.

Some would even say it was a fairy-tale.

But in sport – and sometimes in life too – it helps if you can *BELIEVE ANYTHING IS POSSIBLE*.

And that's the way it has been for a young Queenslander who was born just eleven months after Billy Moore thundered into footy folklore.

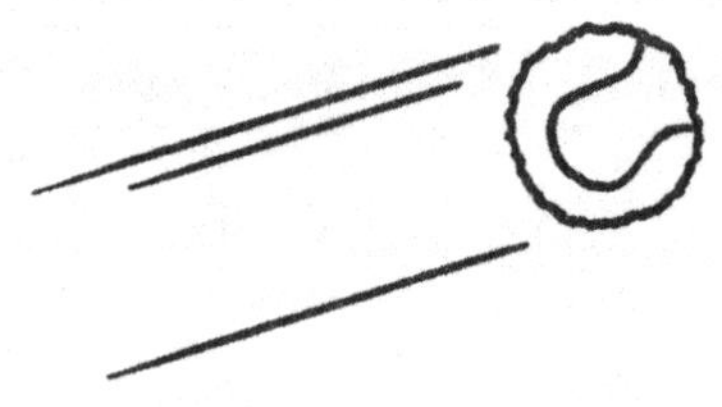

Ashleigh (Ash) Jacinta Barty arrived in this world on 24 April, 1996, a year that had already seen Australia swear-in a new prime minister, John Howard.

(But don't be alarmed, 'swearing-in' doesn't mean Mr Howard said the types of words that, if you said them, would pack you off to the school principal's office; 'swearing-in' is the official term used when the prime minister says carefully chosen words that are known as an 'Oath of Office'. Like, '*I*, (Insert your name) *do swear that I will well and truly serve the people of Australia in the office of Prime Minister.*')

As it turned out, the amazing person who this book is about would also grow up to well and truly serve.

And volley.

And slice.

And lob.

And smash...

And in doing it all, she *served* the people of Australia in a manner that made us glow with pride and a sense of belonging.

Of course, parents Josie and Robert could never have known the journey that lay ahead for their baby girl and their growing family. Like all families the Barty family history was full of twists and turns of people meeting at different times and places and being shaped by the events around them.

Ash's mum, Josie, is the daughter of English immigrants and her dad, Robert, is a descendant of the Indigenous Australian *Ngarigo* people from the alpine regions of New South Wales and Victoria. The Bartys are a family whose history crosses oceans, lands, and cultures.

When baby Ash was brought home, she turned a family of four into a family of five; Robert and Josie already had daughters, Sarah and Ali. They all lived in a house in the suburb of Springfield in the city of Ipswich, about thirty kilometres west of Queensland's capital city, Brisbane.

Yes, they were Queenslanders!

(Actually, Queenslanders are also known as Banana Benders because they grow a lot of... yes, you guessed it. Pineapples. Just kidding!)

It wasn't at all surprising that sport became part of Ash's life because her parents were both exceptional golfers. But driving a pimpled ball down a fairway wasn't what caught Ash's eye (and hand).

However, there was still a connection with golf.

Or kind of!

But to understand that connection we've got to go back 100-or-so years to when there was a boy in the country town of Bowral in New South Wales. A keen cricketer, he practised by hitting a golf ball with a stump against a curved brick tank-stand at his family home. His name was Donald Bradman. Not only would he become Australia's greatest cricketer (born 1908, died 2001), he will always be known as one of our greatest ever Australians.

Now, fast forward the clock to when Ash was a girl, and she practised quite a bit like the young Bradman before her had done. She hit a tennis ball with a wooden racquet against an outside wall of her home.

K-toink-whack

K-toink-whack

K-toink-whack

K-toink-whack

K-toink-whack

K-toink-whack

K-toink-whack

K-toink-whack

K-toink-whack...

Hour after hour after hour.

Just before she turned five years old, Ash was taken by her parents to have a hit at the West Brisbane Tennis Centre, and she immediately made one of the coaches, Jim Joyce, take notice. At an age at which many children are better at catching imaginary butterflies than hitting balls, Ash showed remarkable hand-eye co-ordination and focus.

So, she began training with Jim. And then she turned five years old, and six, and seven and eight and...

But how good was good?

And would that good be good enough to see Ash grow up to travel the world and take on the world's best?

And if she did, could she possibly be as good as those previous Australian tennis players who became legends of their sport? Those legends included a red-headed Queenslander (yes, another one!) nicknamed "Rocket". Can you remember the name of the arena you read about in Chapter One? If you can't, go back and have a look now...We'll all wait for you.

Waiting! Waiting! Waiting!

tick, tick, tick

Great, welcome back. Did you find it?

That's right: *Rod Laver Arena*, which is named after a brilliant left-hander who dominated global tennis in the 1960's.

Rod Laver was born in Rockhampton, central Queensland, in 1938. A former World Number One, he is the only player in history to win the *Grand Slam* twice, which he did in 1962 and 1969.

Throughout his extraordinary career he won more than 20 major international tennis titles playing singles, doubles and mixed doubles.

That's a lot of trophies! And a lot of cabinets to put them in!

Then, in the following decade, along came a player who, well, let's be honest… many Australians fell in love with. Evonne Goolagong Cawley. Those who saw her play will never forget her.

Evonne Goolagong was born in Griffith, in the Riverina region of NSW, in 1951. She grew up in nearby Barellan, just a small town – a pinprick on the map really.

In what is a familiar Australian story, she practised hitting a ball against walls; except she didn't have a stump or a racquet – she used a piece of wood with a shaped handle from a fruit box.

From a girl who dreamt of winning Wimbledon, Evonne grew up to become a World Number One and won more than a dozen major international tennis titles playing singles, doubles and mixed doubles.

Evonne is a *Wiradjuri* woman, and sadly there were times during her career when she encountered racism. In 2005, the Evonne Goolagong Foundation was established to promote better health, education, and employment opportunities for young Indigenous people.

Among many awards she has received, Evonne was named Australian of the Year in 1971, and in 2018 she was given the *International Tennis Federation's* most prestigious honour, the *Philipe Chatrier Award* for her tireless commitment to tennis and community.

So, could a little girl from Ipswich follow successfully in the footsteps of such giants?

At least part of the answer lay with a single, small word.

CHAPTER THREE

THE WORLD IS HER CLASSROOM

When you first start playing a sport, you are taught the fundamentals, which are the basics that help you build a foundation on which you can add more intricate skills as you develop.

For example, in tennis a coach might say –

"Watch the ball all the way onto your racquet!"

Once you have mastered that fundamental, you might be taught how to play a specific shot, such as a forehand or backhand. And on and on your development goes. And it all begins with fundamentals.

Now, have a close look at the beginning of that word:

F–U–N–D–A–M–E–N–T–A–L–S.

What do you see?

Most importantly, the first three letters spell **FUN!**

And FUN is what playing sport should be.

Coach Jim Joyce knew this as he helped guide Ash through her earliest playing years. Jim also emphasised the importance of happiness and being a nice person who respected others and earned respect.

Good on you Jim!

Obviously, there are other ingredients needed to make a successful tennis player.

K-toink-whack

K-toink-whack

K-toink-whack

K-toink-whack

K-toink-whack

K-toink-whack...

Whether it's hitting a ball against a wall, a tank-stand, or anything else that you might choose, there are no short-cuts to becoming better and better and better at tennis, or any other sport for that matter.

You must work hard, concentrate, believe, and

As she developed, and her talent showed what she was capable of, Ash started playing against boys who were much older than her, and then she started playing against men. It was a huge difference, like comparing a freckle to a crater on the moon!

But Ash already seemed to be creating her own orbital path that was growing more and more powerful!

Among many other successes, she was a member of the Queensland Primary Schools team that won the Bruce Cup, a national competition named after Queensland politician, Henry Bruce.

(Coincidentally, Rod Laver also played in the Bruce Cup, in 1952, but back then it was an Under 15s competition.)

Ash also turned heads when she won the Australian Under 12s Hardcourt Singles Championship, in 2008, at Melbourne Park.

You could say that winning tournaments came easily to her, but you'd be wrong because winning takes a **TRUCKLOAD** of determination and dedication.

And it also seemed that Ash could have used a truck, or at least a ute to hold all her trophies! There's no need to mention them all here, but we can say that Ash won tournaments and accolades as frequently as some of us might collect Pokemon cards!

Ash's trophies and medals

Although Ash still managed to attend her local school, Woodcrest State College, there were times when tennis took her away from her classroom and schoolmates. Eventually, her rapid rise with the racquet meant textbooks gave way to passports, and Ash was introduced to overseas travel under the supervision of various tennis officials and coaches.

In 2009, when she was just thirteen, she played junior tournaments in The Netherlands, France, Germany, Belgium, and New Zealand.

Then in 2010, she played her first professional tournament – **yes that's right, professional!**

It was a $25,000 event in... drumroll please... **Ipswich!** (Ash's hometown.)

Unfortunately, she lost in the first round.

Then in her next pro competition, in Mount Gambier, South Australia, she won three consecutive matches to advance to a semi-final before losing to her Brazilian opponent.

Getting better.

Go ASH!

By then, Ash had also represented Australia at junior international competitions in the Czech Republic and Mexico.

In her tournaments and travels, she was discovering that the world could be as far away as twenty hours on a plane, or as close as the other side of the net. What an eye-opener for a young Aussie teenager.

And those eyes never opened more widely than during a short trip to a city renowned for its glamour and glitz, its razzle and ritz, ***its over-the-top-flash-of-fortunes-and-fun-and-spotlights-and-stars-and-oh-my-goodness-we-are-in-Las-Vegas-U-S-of-A-can-you-believe-this-is-actually-happening-dude-that's-awesome!***

That's right, somewhere among all her competitions, Ash found time to spend a week in "Vegas" as a member of the prestigious Adidas development team.

This was no standard training camp, but a priceless opportunity to train with highly respected coach and former player Darren Cahill, the Australian who had previously coached one of the all-time superstars of tennis, Andre Agassi.

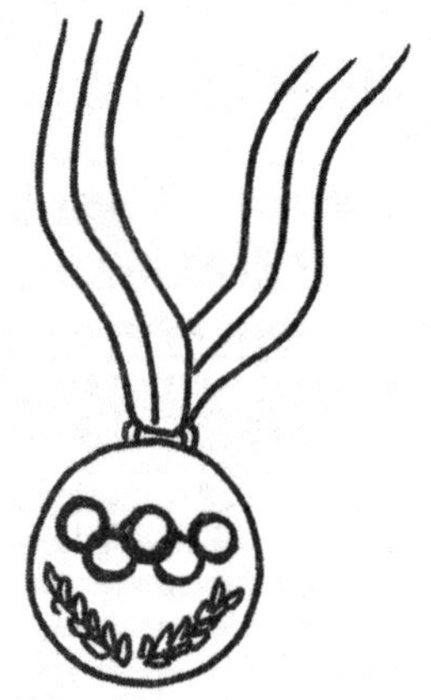

Agassi started his career as a long-haired kid who looked like a lead-singer in a 1980's rock-band, and he finished his career as bald as a light-globe; in between those stages of hairdos (and hairdon'ts) he made headlines nearly everywhere he went.

He won eight major singles championships *and* an Olympic gold medal.

Plus, he also happened to marry an all-time **MEGASTAR** of tennis, Germany's Steffi Graf, who won twenty-two major singles titles, which included a *Grand Slam* in 1988.

Oh, and she also won gold, silver, and bronze medals at the Olympics.

So, you could imagine how excited Ash must have been when she met the power-couple!

Ash also went to a baseball game with Steffi.

Forget striking out, Ash struck it lucky.

Big time!

And then came 2011... It's time to say wow, again.

But before we get to the enormous moment of this year, we need a little background.

In elite sport, people sometimes talk about

POTENTIAL.

Put simply, it means if you are recognised as having some type of ability – such as playing sport, painting, or singing – people might suggest that your ability could be developed into something useful, and it might bring you lots of success.

However, there's a massive difference between HAVING potential and FULFILLING potential.

Put yourself in the shoes of a teenage Ash Barty.

You're playing well, working hard, winning, impressing important people, and that word **POTENTIAL** starts popping up in conversations about you. Expectations are high. Not just climb-a-ladder-type-of-high but launch-yourself-into-space-type-of-high.

And that can put pressure on you. Lots of it! So, how would *you* cope?

Thankfully Ash had many good people supporting her, and although there were times when she got very homesick, she still loved playing tennis.

And as for fulfilling potential?

Well, 2011 gave a hint of what was to come.

That was the year that Ash stepped up to compete in all four *Junior* Grand Slam events which hosted the world's best players aged from fourteen to eighteen years old. The events were held at the same venues and at the same time as the main Open tournaments where crowds flocked to watch the greats, including Serena and Venus Williams, Roger Federer, Rafael Nadal, and Novak Djokovic.

Unfortunately, it was a tough beginning for Ash. She was only fourteen when she lost in the first round at the Australian (Junior) Open.

Tough.

And then, a month after her fifteenth birthday, she won just one match at the French (Junior) Open on the red clay courts of Roland Garros, Paris.

Better...

Then, it was on to...

Courts of brilliant green lawn mown in exquisite strips.

WIMBLEDON.

Strawberries and cream.

WIMBLEDON.

Royalty and movie stars.

WIMBLEDON!

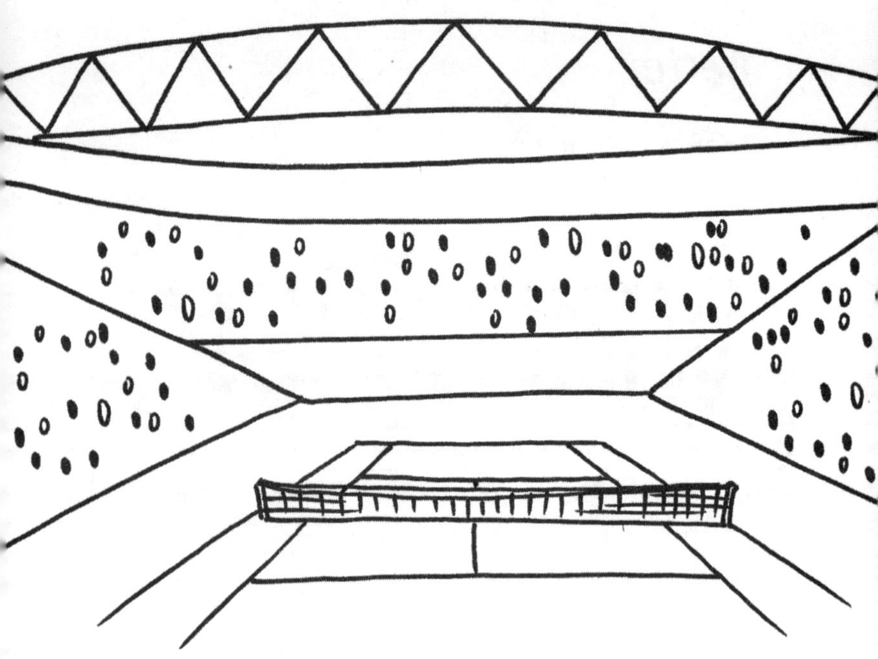

It may surprise you that Wimbledon is not the official name of the tournament. In fact, Wimbledon is a suburb in south-west London, England. But it is home to the *All England Lawn Tennis and Croquet Club* that hosts the oldest tennis tournament in the world, The Championships, which were first held in 1877. Over the years, this tournament has become known by most of us as Wimbledon.

Playing at Wimbledon was an enormous honour for a shy teenager who was a very long way from Ipswich.

Ash was the twelfth seed, and one of sixty-four players in the Junior Girls' Singles. A scan along the competition draw was an exercise in geography. There were players from Ukraine, Bulgaria, Sweden, Brazil, Germany, USA, Japan, Croatia, Serbia, The Netherlands, Ecuador,

Paraguay, and more. All had dreams. But at the end of the week-long tournament, there could be only one champion.

Ash won her first match.

Straight sets.

A promising start.

Second match.

Again, a straight sets win.

Looking good.

Third match.

Tough.

Won the first set. Lost the second. And...victory in the third.

Well done.

Fourth match.

A quarter-final. Only eight players left.

Take a breath.

Another straight sets win.

COME ON!

Fifth match. A semi-final.

Just go and have fun.

Do it! Do it! Do it!

DONE IT!

6–4, 6–1

Sixth match.

WIMBLEDON!

WOOAHH!

THE FINAL.

One of the world's most prestigious sports events.

WIMBLEDON!

The history, the traditions, the fame.

WIMBLEDON!

Names and deeds that last forever.

WIMBLEDON!

At just fifteen years old, Ash was about to face a final at Wimbledon… It would be a career-defining moment for the young Australian, number twelve seed, Ashleigh Barty.

She was about to face the number three seed, Irina Kromacheva, sixteen years old, from Russia.

Kromacheva started brilliantly, and she looked likely to win the first set, racing to a **4–1** lead.

But in tennis, you can't unhappen what has happened, and nor can you control the future. You can only control the very moment you are in.

Each step, each backswing, each connection your racquet makes with the ball.

Live in the moment. And try your very best in that moment. And the next moment too.

And the one after that..

AGAIN. AGAIN. AGAIN.

Ash fought back to win the set, **7–5**.

The second set was even tighter. Stroke after stroke, point after point, moment after moment.

Until...

Well...

Precious few players will ever have the thrill and privilege of winning on centre court at the *All England Lawn Tennis and Croquet Club* in Wimbledon. But on 3 July 2011, the chair umpire said "**7–5**, **7–6**," and fifteen-year-old Ash Barty became one of them.

The numbers told the score, but in the days that followed, different numbers told a deeper story. Ash had become the first Indigenous Australian to win at Wimbledon since Evonne Goolagong Cawley was crowned Women's Singles Champion in 1980.

(She had also won the title in 1971).

In the media, many comparisons between Evonne and Ash had already been made. By then, the two had met, and they'd established a strong connection. They were people from different eras, but they were so powerfully linked through tennis, heritage, and culture.

As time passed, their relationship would only grow stronger, and as it did, there was a question that couldn't be avoided: Could Ash follow in Evonne's legendary footsteps and win the Women's Singles title at Wimbledon?

Only time would tell.

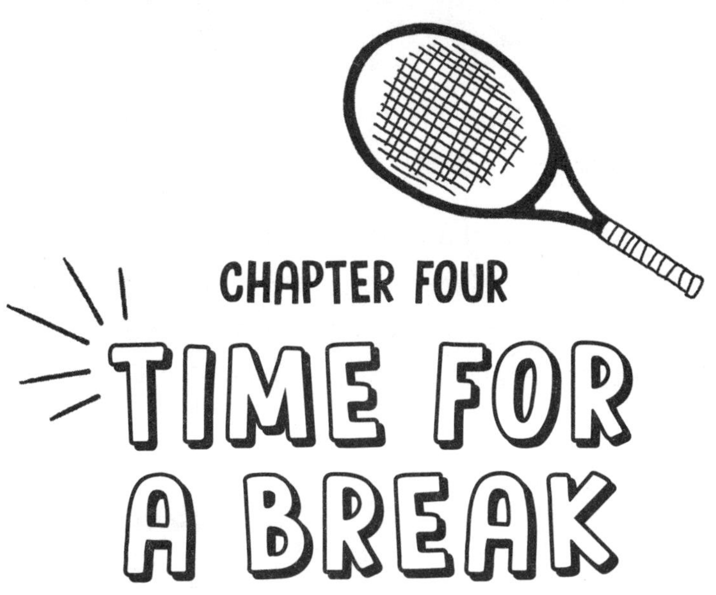

CHAPTER FOUR

TIME FOR A BREAK

Have you heard of William Shakespeare? Maybe. Maybe not. Either way, it's likely you'll study him at some point during your school years.

He was born way back in 1564 in England, and his name and deeds will live forever. He wrote plays and poetry, and his works are considered some of the most important ever written. Perhaps you have heard of *Romeo and Juliet*? Or *Macbeth*?

Okay, by now you are probably asking:

What does William Shakespeare have to do with Ash Barty?

Good question! So, let's get to the answer. In one of his plays *King Henry the Fourth (Part One)* which is about battles for territory and power, Shakespeare wrote this line for King Henry:

It's strange language, isn't it? But you must remember that people spoke very differently in those times. If we try to put it into modern day speech, King Henry was saying something kinda like:

Winning is totally sick. Nothing is bad if you win.

Let's be honest, good old King Hen was right.

WINNING IS TOTALLY SICK!

We all like to win, don't we? It can give us a buzz, makes us feel good about ourselves and our teammates, and we get a bit of a pep in our step, a glide in our stride.

And that's the way Australian tennis was feeling in 2011. Not only did Ash win Junior Wimbledon, but another Aussie, seventeen-year-old Luke Saville, claimed the Boys' title.

Two months later, neither player could reproduce their results at the Junior US Open in New York (although Ash made it all the way to the Semi-Finals), but Australia still had reason to cheer.

In the Women's Open Singles Final, Samantha Stosur beat Serena Williams. Awesome!

Now, here's a quick challenge for you? See if you can fill in the spaces below.

In triumphing at the 2011 US Open, Samantha Stosur became the first Australian woman to win a Grand Slam Event Singles title since

.... **won at**

.... **in 1980.**

(Hint: the name of the person and the venue are mentioned in the previous chapter. If you're still not sure, maybe you can peek at the very end of this chapter.)

Got it? Okay, on we go.

So, 2011 was an exciting time to be part of tennis down-under. The future looked bright, and Ash was doing her part. In October, she was a member of the three-player Australian team that won the Junior Fed Cup, and by the end of the year she was Number Two Junior Girl in the World according to the official rankings of the International Tennis Federation.

In very simple terms, a player can earn ranking points at various tournaments, and the better they play, the more points they earn.

So, let's stop for a moment and think about Ash's ranking.

tick, tick, tick

(Stop and think time)

(Stop and think time)

(Stop and think time)

(Stop and think time)

Okay, now ask yourself how impressive that ranking is?

NUMBER TWO.

Not in Springfield.

Not in Brisbane.

Not in Queensland.

Not In Australia.

Not in the Pacific region.

Not in the Southern Hemisphere.

But...

That's cool.

Let's try looking at it this way.

Imagine if you filled an empty bottle with hundreds-and-thousands, and each tiny one represents a tennis player. Then you pour those hundreds-and-thousands all over the kitchen table. Then you pick up just one of those tiny balls of sugar. That is the Number One ranked player. And then you pick up a second ball. That's Number Two.

Now, look at all those other hundreds-and-thousands that are still on the table; they are the players below Ash, and Ash knew how they felt because only two years earlier (2009), she was Number 1876.

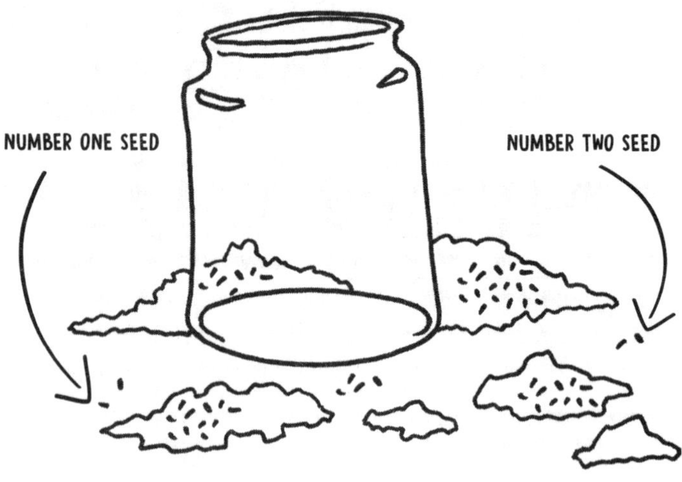

But no matter how *sweet* (yes, it's a terrible pun!) her climb up the Junior ranks may have been, it counted for nothing when Ash took the next significant *and intimidating* step of her young career.

In 2012, at the age of just fifteen, she made her debut at the Australian Open!

She was just a kid among the super-powered giants of her sport, including Serena Williams (thirty years old), Kim Clijsters (twenty-eight years old) and Maria Sharapova (twenty-four years old).

Some people might say that hardly seems fair, but that was the reality of elite professional tennis, and it was the path that Ash had to take if she truly wanted to rise to the top. She lost in the first round to twenty-two-year-old Anna Tatishvili from Georgia, and she was also knocked out in the first round of the French Open, and Wimbledon. (She did not play the US open that year.)

Every match was a learning experience for a school-age girl who had discovered her classroom was the world itself.

Soon enough, Ash left behind Junior tournaments, and embarked on a journey of winning and losing (*and always learning*) in Australia and overseas.

Players and commentators sometimes say such journeys are **ROLLERCOASTER RIDES**.

Up, down, a twist here, a drop there **WHOOOOAH. HANG ON!**

If you have been on a real rollercoaster ride, you might know how scary they can be, but...

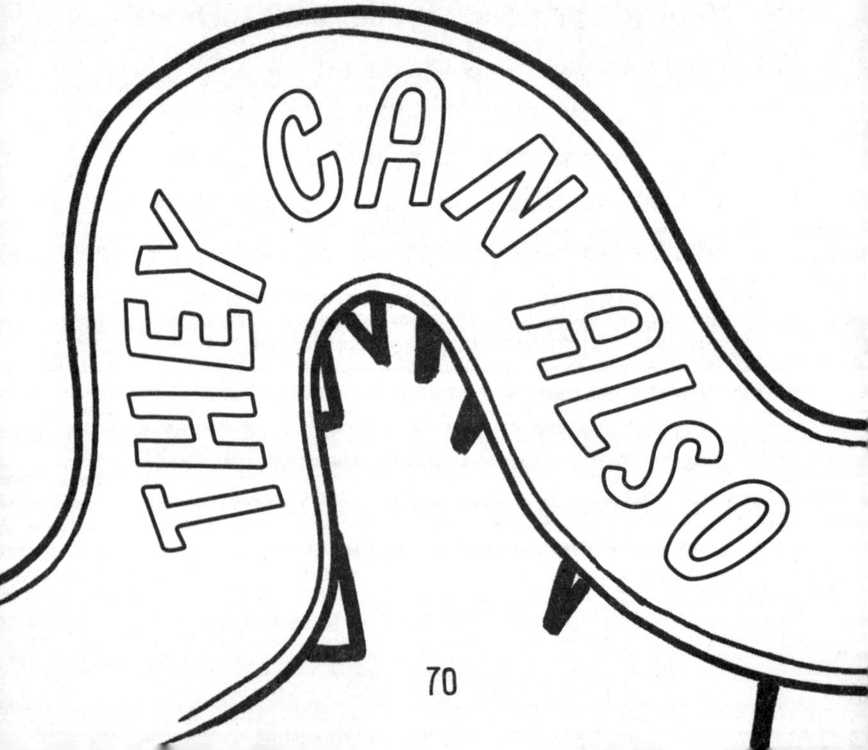

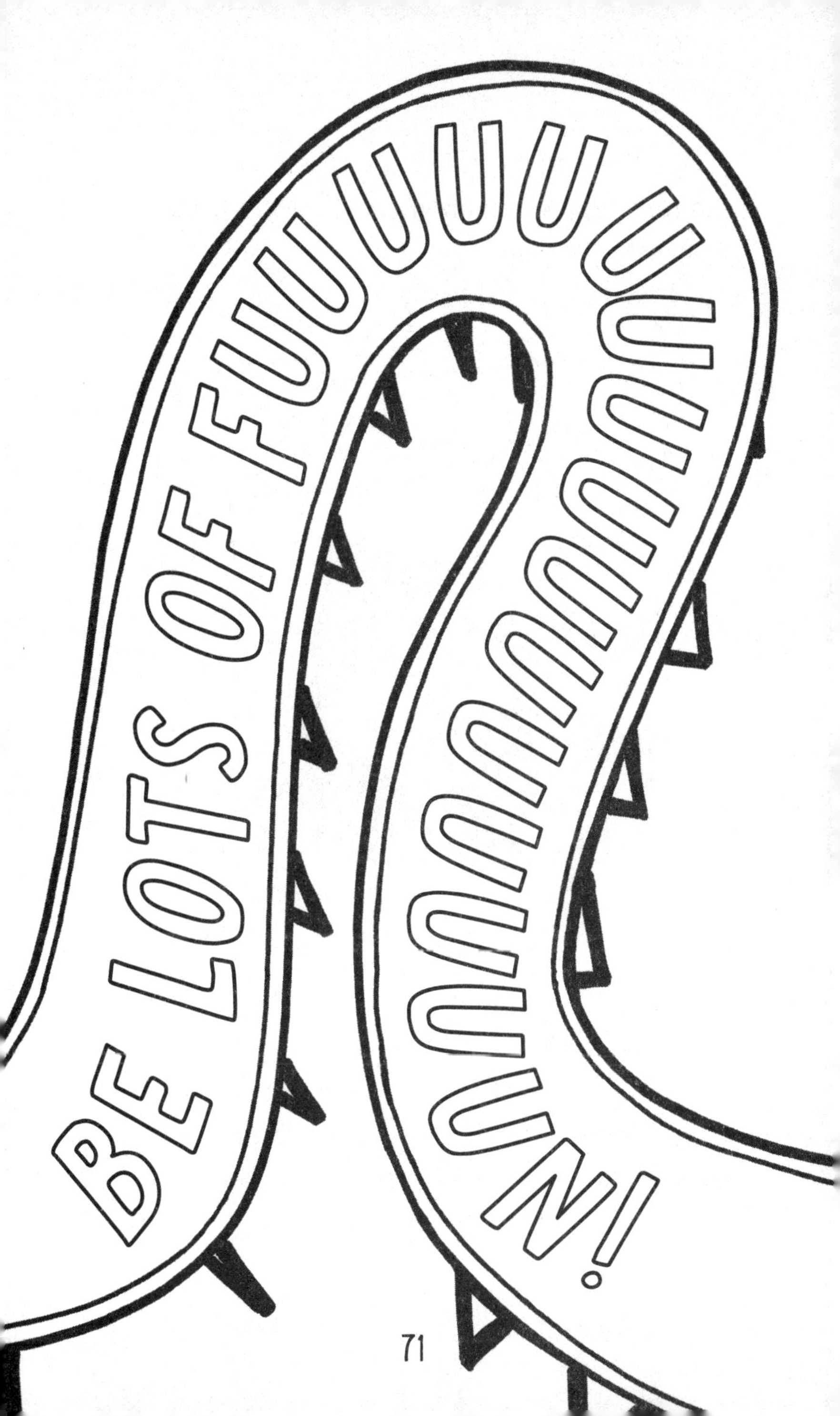
BE LOTS OF FUUUUUUUUUUUUUUUUN!

And that's the way Ash found it to be when she teamed up with another Australian to play Women's Doubles.

Casey Dellacqua was eleven years older than Ash, in fact, she was so much older that she'd been born before the World Wide Web (WWW) came into existence. But let's put those *W's* to a different use.

When it came to the Dellacqua/Barty combination, it was more a case of

WIN! WIN! WIN!

In 2013, they won the Birmingham Classic in England, and they also finished runners-up at the Australian Open and Wimbledon.

WWW?

WHAT! WONDERFUL! WORK!

In 2013 Ash also won her first Singles match at a Grand Slam event when she beat twenty-eight-year-old Lucie Hradecka from the Czech Republic at the French Open. She also won in the opening round at the US Open.

At one point, the world's major women's professional tennis organisation, the Women's Tennis Association (WTA), ranked Ash 129th. At seventeen years of age, she had many reasons to be thrilled with her progress, but...

The life of a professional tennis player can be VERY CHALLENGING...

This is what Ash's life became:

Leave home.

Leave family.

Fly to the other side of the world.

Book into a hotel.

Ring home.

Eat.

Sleep.

Wake up.

Go to training.

Return to hotel.

Ring home.

Eat. Sleep.

Wake up.

Go to training.

Return to hotel. Ring home. Eat. Sleep.

Wake up. Play a match. Win.

Return to hotel. Ring home.

Eat. Sleep. Wake up. Go to training.

Return to hotel. Ring home. Eat. Sleep.

Play a match. Lose.

Leave hotel.

Fly to another country.

Book into a hotel.

Ring home...

Day after day.

Week after week.

Month after month.

The year ends. Another one begins.

On you go. Again.

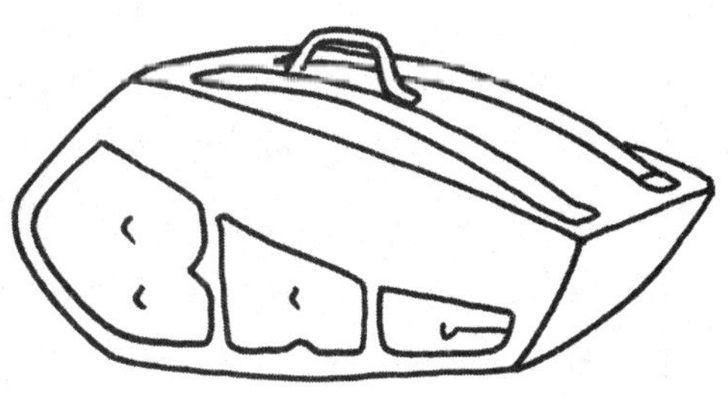

Ash's rollercoaster had been replaced by a merry-go-round that rarely ever stopped!

What a difficult way for a kid to live.

Ash wasn't the first girl to go through this and women's professional tennis has a long history of having teenage players. In 1990, American Jennifer Capriati was only thirteen years old when she turned professional!

And in more recent times, fifteen-year-old American, Cori Gauff, became the youngest ever player to qualify for Wimbledon. She beat thirty-nine-year-old five-time Wimbledon Singles champion, Venus Williams, in the first round, and won two further matches.

However, don't start thinking YOU might be able to jump onto the professional circuit at any age you like because there are strict age-eligibility rules in place.

In 1994, the Women's Tennis Association decided the earliest age that a girl can turn professional is fourteen years old. And players aged between fourteen and seventeen can only play limited numbers of tournaments. It is only when they turn eighteen that the restrictions are lifted and the girls can play as many tournaments as they like (as long as they can qualify for them!)

For boys the minimum playing age is fourteen but they can participate in an unlimited number of tournaments when they turn sixteen, two years earlier than girls.

Luckily Ash had supportive people around her during this time, including her coach, Jason Stoltenberg (who was a former Wimbledon Men's Singles Semi-finalist) but the heartfelt help wasn't enough.

Ash had cried too much and been homesick and lonely too many times.

Just weeks after losing her first-round match at the 2014 US Open, Ash made a

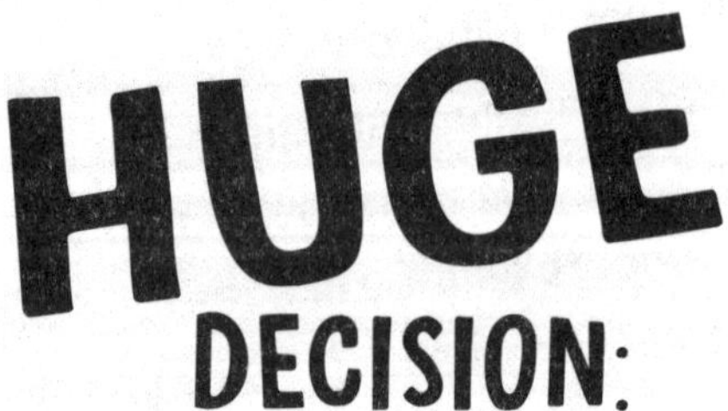

she would stop playing professional tennis.

Simple as that.

This was her official statement:

> Since returning from the US Open my team and I have decided that right now it is best for me to take a break from professional tennis. Obviously, this has been a very difficult decision with the Australian summer coming up but after a lot of thought we feel this is the right decision. I've enjoyed some incredible experiences on the tennis tour and would like to thank my coach, Jason, and the team at TA (Tennis Australia) for all of its hard work and support throughout my journey so far.

(Tennis Australia Media Release, September 19, 2014)

But was Ash's tennis career finished forever?

No-one, including Ash, knew the answer.

(Oh, by the way... The missing words on page 65 are Evonne Goolagong Cawley and Wimbledon.)

Hiatus.

That's a strange looking word, isn't it?

Pronounced: *High-ay-tuss*

(Don't make too big a deal of the 'u' sound, though)

It means: **A break or interruption in continuity.**

(If you can use it correctly in a sentence you might impress your teachers, but perhaps it's best not to say: *I don't think I need to go to school, so I'm taking a hiatus from it.*)

Ash's **hiatus** from professional tennis began in late September 2014.

Ash was eighteen years old.

Tennis had given her **SO MUCH**, but it had also taken away from her...

Ash hadn't had a typical childhood. In fact, it's fair to say that because of her devotion to tennis, she had missed out on being a kid in so many ways. Like, playing tag in the playground at school recess; riding a bike to a friend's house on a Saturday afternoon; going shopping with the parents and sneakily putting a block of chocolate in the trolley...

Simple pleasures. Kid pleasures.

After beginning her hiatus, Ash found ways to relax.

How do *you* do that? Do you walk your dog? Or shoot some hoops in the local park? Maybe you play the guitar? Or play *Minecraft* with your friends? Or maybe you lock your little brother out of your bedroom so you can listen to your favourite playlist without being interrupted?

But for Ash, fishing was the way to relax.

Throw a line into the water and get lost in the moment.

Aaaaaaah, how peaceful. Not a worry in the world.

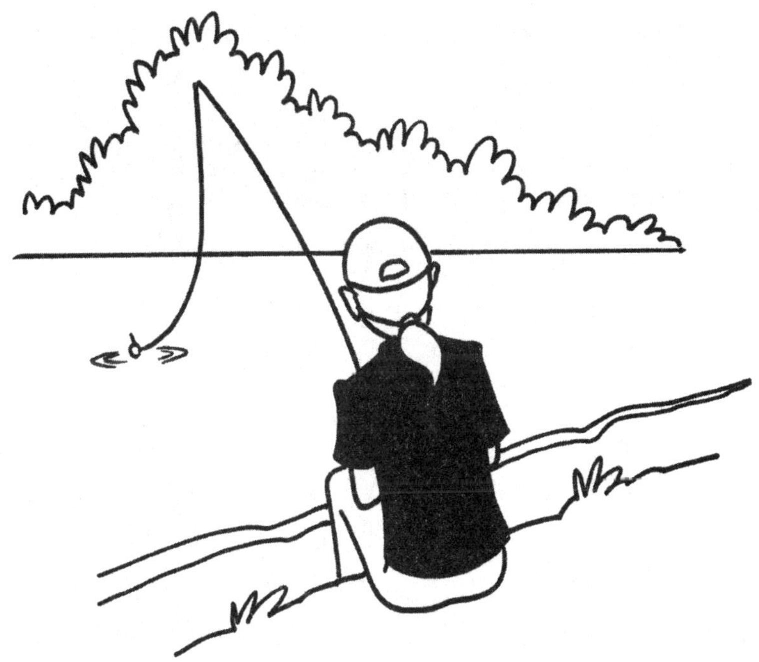

And then there was watching her favourite AFL team, Richmond.

Carn the Tigers!

Most importantly, Ash spent lots of time with her family. Precious time.

She also helped her first coach, Jim Joyce, train the next generation of youngsters, and much older players too. But Ash didn't seem to have an immediate desire to return herself to the long hours of K-toink-whack, k-toink-whack, k-toink-whack...

She was impressing people with her ability to whack a golf ball, but it was another type of ball – the six stitcher – that intrigued her more.

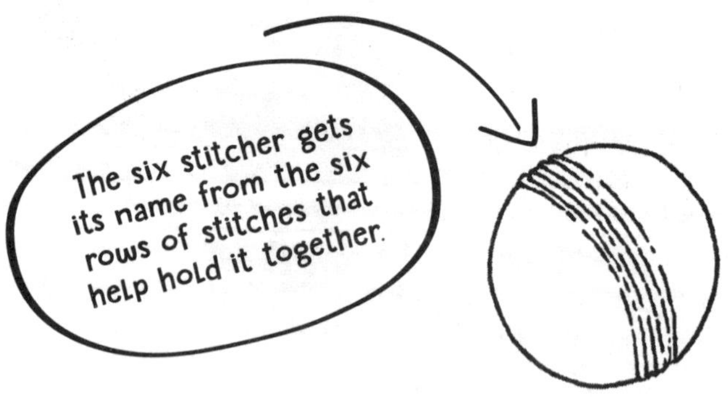

In one of life's unexpected twists, Ash had the opportunity to excel in another sport!

She was invited to talk to the Australian women's cricket team about her experiences as an athlete. They also shared their experiences of playing cricket at an international level and the thought of playing a team sport seemed to really appeal to Ash.

Cricket is very different to the intense and often individual nature of professional tennis.

In cricket, people play hard, but there's also time to have a chat on the field, to share jokes, and to support teammates during the good times and the bad. Then after the game, players often stay at the field and talk or go and socialise at a club.

Cricket seemed to be about togetherness.

Ash quickly discovered she thrived in the team environment!

She joined the Western Suburbs District Cricket Club that played in the Queensland Women's Premier Grade competition, but her first match in the 2015-16 season was no fairy-tale. She was caught and bowled for a duck (no runs) and she didn't take any wickets while bowling two overs of medium pace.

However, she did take a catch!

In her second match, **what a difference!**

As an opening batter Ash slammed 63 runs off 60 balls to help her team to an easy T-20 win. Her innings included two 6s and anyone who has ever hit a 6 knows the feeling it can give.

Ash played a key role in the Wests' team all season.

In one match she blasted 107 runs off 66 balls, and later, she top-scored with 37 in the Grand Final.

Wests won. The team celebrated.

***The Team!* Ash loved it.**

By then, Ash had also played for Queensland in the Women's National Cricket League 50-overs competition, and here's a question that you can put in your next *Kahoot* quiz:

Tick, tick, tick goes the timer.

HOW INCREDIBLE IS THAT?

The match was played in front of 1500 people at Melbourne's Junction Oval, which is a grand historic ground, established in 1856.

So, as women's cricket launched a thrilling new era, it was a case of the old and the new together.

Playing for the **Brisbane Heat**, Ash scored 39 runs off 27 balls, but it wasn't enough to stop the **Melbourne Stars** from winning.

If you want another Kahoot question, try this one:

Who top scored in the first ever WBBL match in Australia?

ANSWER:
Meg Lanning
(Melbourne Stars)

Meg, the Australian Captain, and one of the true superstars of world cricket, scored 90 runs in that first ever WBBL match.

Life can be full of mysteries and magic!

Do you think Meg and Ash would ever have imagined they'd play a professional cricket match against each other?

I wonder how Meg would go if she had to play tennis against Ash?

(Perhaps it would be close if Meg demanded that Ash play while wearing gloves, pads, and a helmet!)

Cricket and tennis require many different skills, but there is one obvious similarity between them: the need for hand-eye co-ordination.

Without being too scientific, hand-eye co-ordination shows how astonishing the human body and mind can be.

Try this exercise for yourself: throw a ball against a wall, then catch it. Try it a few times if you like.

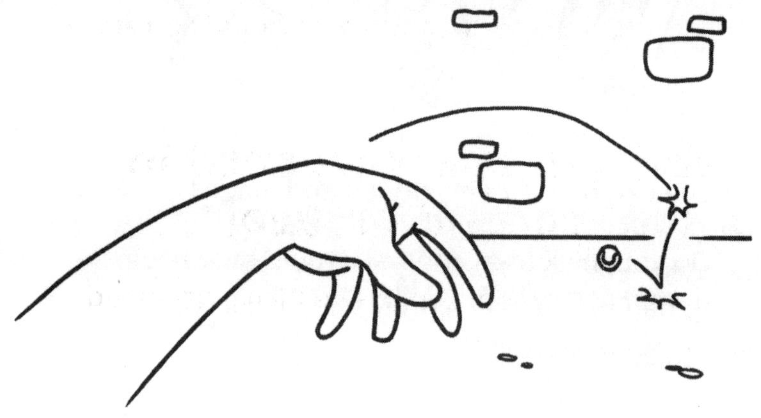

Now, think about what just happened.

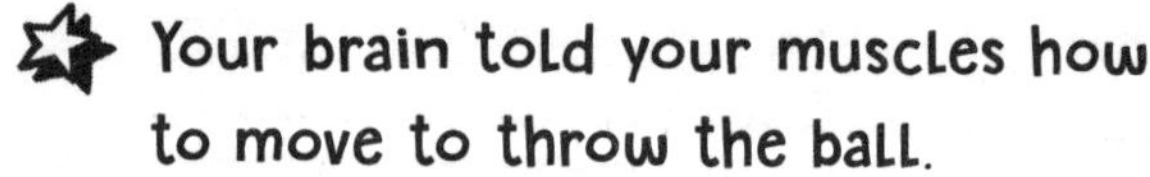

- Your brain told your muscles how to move to throw the ball.

- Your eyes watched the ball.
- Your brain processed what your eyes were seeing.

- Your brain sent signals via neural pathways which reached your muscles and told them to move in a way that enabled your hands to be in a specific place to catch the ball.
- At the same time as giving these other signals, your brain also told your fingers to wrap around the ball at an exact moment.

And all that happened in a split second or two!

That's much more impressive than high-speed internet connections!

Ash is not the first athlete to turn her hand-eye coordination to more than one elite sport and she is in good company with some other amazing Australian champions!

What about **Ellyse Perry** who made her debut as a bowling all-rounder for the Australian Women's cricket team in a 50-overs match against New Zealand, in July 2007, and then only twelve days later she played her very first game for the Australian Women's soccer team, the Matildas, against Hong Kong.

Playing in the midfield, she scored a goal in the game's second minute. And this is the craziest thing of all... she was only sixteen years old.

There are plenty of other multi-talented athletes too, like **Nicole Richardson** who won a bronze medal as a member of the Australian Women's softball team at the 1996 Atlanta Olympics and then, six years later, was part of Australia's gold medal winning netball team at the Commonwealth Games in Manchester!

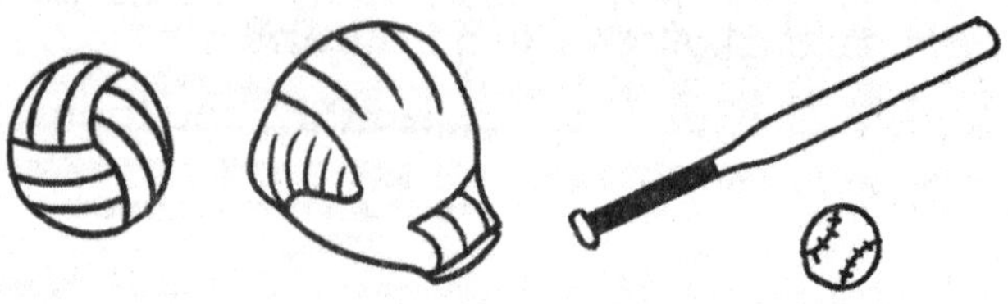

There's also **Nova Peris**, an Indigenous Australian who won gold with the Hockeyroos at the 1996 Atlanta Olympics, and then a year later claimed two gold medals as a sprinter at the Commonwealth Games in Kuala Lumpur!

Or if you look even further back, you'll come across the deeds of **Reginald Leslie 'Snowy' Baker** who made headlines in a swag of sports in the early 1900s. Snowy played rugby union for Australia in 1904 and then represented Australia at the 1908 Olympics in London, competing in both swimming and diving and winning a silver medal in middle weight boxing.

And let's not forget international athletes.

Remember, **Usain *Lightning* Bolt** from Jamaica? Now, he was fast. Blink-and-you-miss-him fast! An eight-time Olympic gold medallist and multi-world record breaker who owned the track when he sprinted.

But I bet you didn't know that he played a little bit of professional soccer for the Central Coast Mariners in Australia? It's true! Look him up. It's a fascinating story.

There are plenty of others too. Go on, do some searching and make your own list.

You never know, one day you might be on it!

In all, Ash played nine games for the Brisbane Heat and they finished sixth in the 2015-16 WBBL season.

It was a fun-filled time of Ash's life, but the hiatus also gave Ash a lot of time to think, including about her future...

In February 2016, the results of that thinking saw a certain multi-talented athlete put down the cricket bat and pick up a ???

Can you guess?

CHAPTER SIX

SHE'S BACK! (WITH A TENNIS RACQUET)

A tennis racquet. The tool of the tennis trade!

Over the years the size, weight and flexibility of racquets has changed in the quest to increase a player's accuracy and speed and to maximise the **SWEET SPOT** where the ball hits the strings.

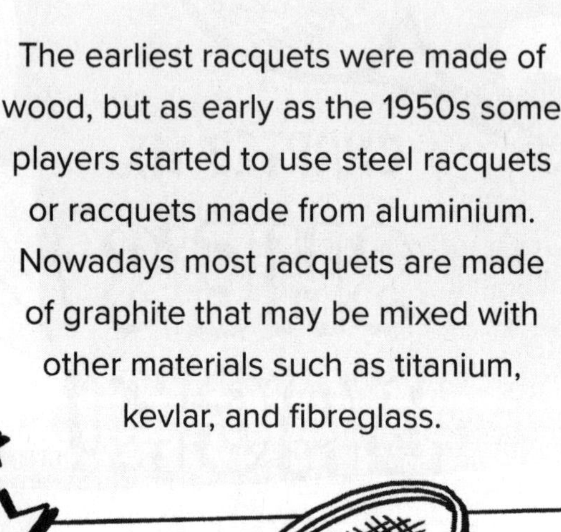

The earliest racquets were made of wood, but as early as the 1950s some players started to use steel racquets or racquets made from aluminium. Nowadays most racquets are made of graphite that may be mixed with other materials such as titanium, kevlar, and fibreglass.

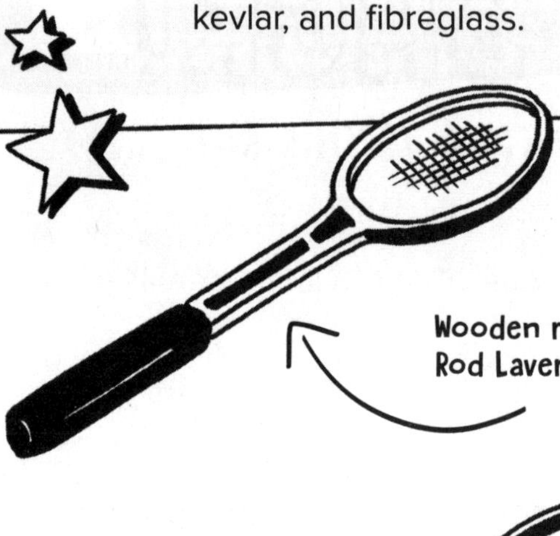

Wooden racquet
Rod Laver, 1960s

Steel racquet of
Evonne Goolagong,
1980

As for the strings... Well, can you believe this? In the 1870's a Frenchman named Pierre Babolat designed strings made from sheep intestines that became known as "natural gut" strings.

These days strings are made from either cattle intestines or synthetic materials and racquets tend to be larger and much lighter than the traditional wooden racquets.

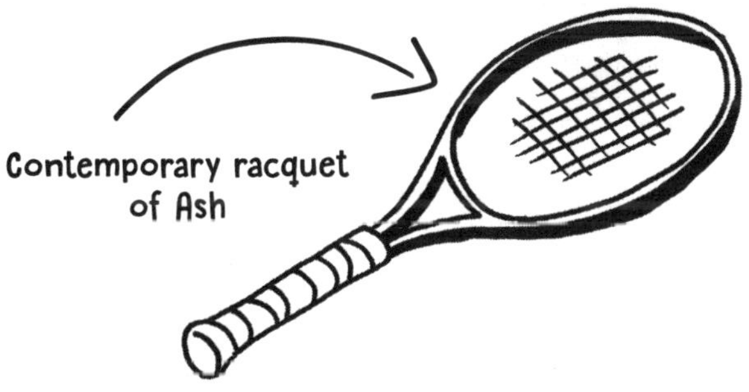

Given enough time, people – just like racquets – change too. And that includes Ash.

She learnt much about herself during her hiatus from tennis, and after nearly one-and-a-half years away from playing competitively, **SHE KNEW SHE WANTED TO RETURN.**

Her time spent with family, friends, teammates, and others had been invaluable; she was more mature than when she'd started her hiatus, and she was better equipped to handle the rollercoasters and merry-go-rounds that lay ahead.

So, in February 2016, she was back on court swinging a racquet and re-building her career.

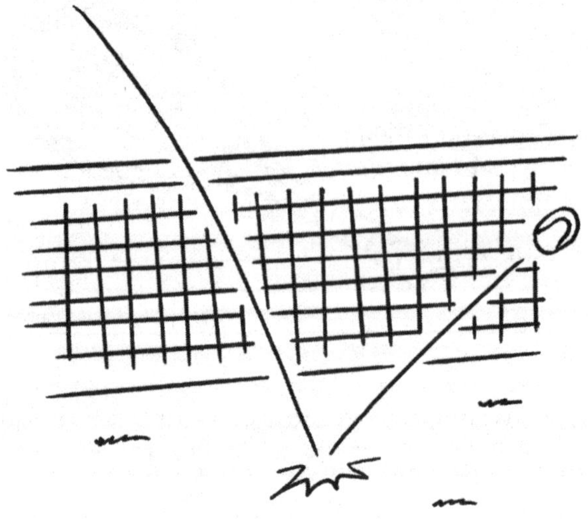

The rest of the year was spent winning and losing and losing and winning.

She played both singles and doubles at various levels, but her playing came at a cost. She suffered an arm injury that troubled her for months before she was back to full strength.

Such is the nature of professional sport that sustaining and overcoming injuries is part of the job. How many football tackles have you seen on TV where a player falls in a screaming heap and then the commentators say:

Oh no, that could be the end of their season?

Tennis can put all sorts of strain on the body from hitting, hurtling, smashing, lunging, tumbling, turning.

Ankles, knees, shoulders, arms, feet, fingers, wrists...

X-rays, scans, operations, stitches, plaster!

It happens. That's tennis. That's sport. And that's life too.

Luckily for Ash, she was able to bounce back quite quickly and if 2016 was a rollercoaster for Ash, then the start of 2017 was a rocket!

And the launchpad was the Australian Open.

10
9
8
7
6
5
4
3
2
1
WE HAVE
LIFT OFF!

After failing to win a Singles match in her previous three attempts, Ash won her first two matches, and she and Casey Dellacqua won three matches before losing in the quarter finals of the Doubles.

Since they'd first met, Ash and Casey had always enjoyed each other's company, and Casey's caring support had played an important role in helping Ash readjust to the professional circuit. Regardless of what happened when they played together, they were already enjoying one of the greatest gifts that any sport can offer:

TENNIS IS THE BEST!

Two months after the Australian Open, Ash competed at the Malaysian Open in Kuala Lumpur, a hot and humid tropical city where the temperature regularly soars above thirty degrees Celsius. The heat radiating off the playing surface means temperatures on court can be even **HOTTER**.

To anyone playing in such an environment, one word which springs to mind is **SWEAT!**

Beads on the forehead, salt stinging the eyes, clammy hands, sticky clothes, and dry, dry throats... all can make physical activity difficult, and at times, uncomfortable.

Tennis players train for all sorts of conditions and they need all kinds of weapons in their armoury.

POWER,
STRENGTH,
SPEED,

AGILITY AND ENDURANCE!

Ash had worked hard to improve all these aspects, and the results showed in the oven-like atmosphere in Kualar Lumpur.

Ash won five matches in a row to claim her first WTA Singles title.

She finished the Final on her serve...

That was a fitting way to move into the Top 100 of WTA rankings in Women's Singles.

By the end of the year, Ash had finished runner-up in two other Finals and she was ranked 17th in the world, climbing all the way from 272nd where she had finished the year before.

What a trajectory!

The rocket was sweeping Ash to heights she'd never known.

Ash continued to wield her racquet successfully the following year. In 2018, she won two Singles tournaments and she celebrated her breakthrough Grand Slam event triumph when she and American Coco Vandeweghe won the Women's Doubles titles at the US Open.

(Sadly, Ash's former Doubles partner and forever-good mate, Casey Dellacqua, had retired from professional tennis earlier in the year. She and Ash last played Doubles together several months earlier when they helped Australia defeat Ukraine in a Fed Cup tie in Canberra.)

The tournament victories that Ash enjoyed in 2017 and 2018 show how just versatile she was becoming – she had won on hard court and grass court, with each surface having distinct characteristics that require different styles of play.

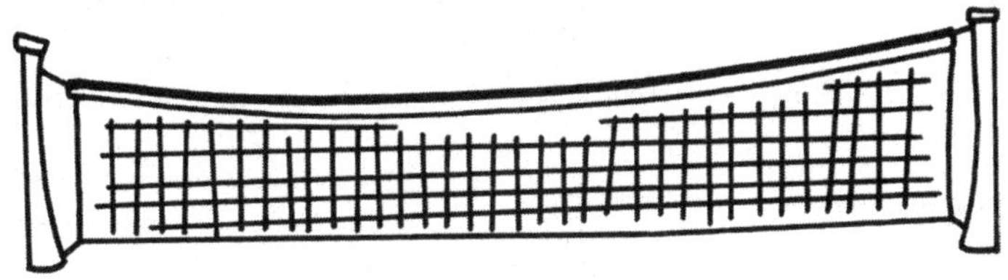

GRASS (WIMBLEDON)

Grass courts are laid on hard-packed soil. They are fast, meaning the ball can come off the surface quickly. The bounce of the ball is affected by how recently the grass has been mown, and the condition of the grass. By the end of the two week-long Wimbledon tournament the grass is worn, so there is variable bounce, meaning the ball may stay low in some parts of the courts, but bounce higher in other sections.

HARD COURT (AUSTRALIAN OPEN AND US OPEN)

Hard Courts are often made from acrylic products that are usually laid on top of concrete or bitumen. Acrylic is a very strong and stiff plastic material. Balls bounce more consistently on hard courts than they do on grass courts, but the speed can vary according to the different types of acrylic materials that are used.

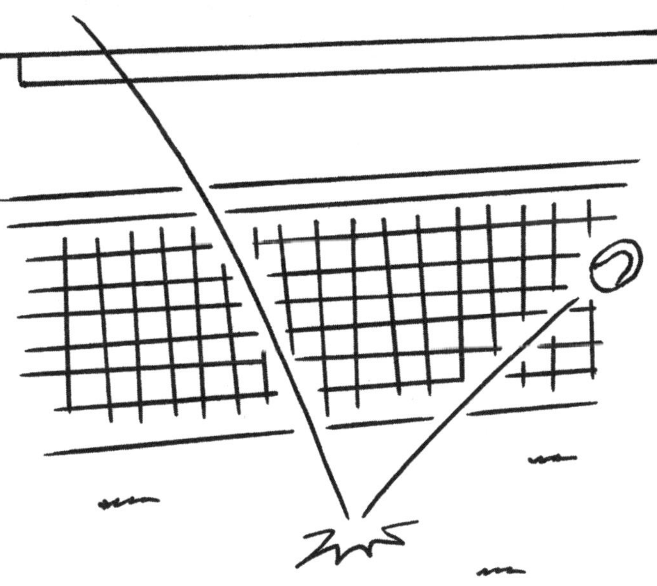

But there is a third type of court in the Grand Slam events and elite tennis players need to be able to adapt their style to succeed in **ALL** conditions.

CLAY COURT (FRENCH OPEN)

Clay courts are made from crushed stone. The finest layer is placed on top. At the French Open, this layer is called "terra battue", which is a red brick dust that is widely known as "the dirt" or "the red stuff." Clay courts are normally slower than other courts and are receptive to spin. Rallies on clay courts can be much longer than on other surfaces, and matches have been known to last for many hours.

Ash finished the year ranked fifteenth in the world in Women's Singles, after wins on both grass and hard courts, but would Ash have the stamina to win on clay?

And could she continue her rise?
And if she did, how high could she go?

Anyone who knows much about rockets knows the sky is the limit!

CHAPTER SEVEN

ON TOP OF THE WORLD

Can you remember what you were doing at the start of 2019? Learning how to round up sheep on nan and pop's farm? Practising scales on the clarinet? Doing a few tail-whips on the mountain bike?

For Ash, the beginning of 2019 saw history repeat itself *two* many times. Yes, yes, that *"two"* is not correct, is it? It should be "too", but bear with me here because it suits the theme!

For the *second* straight year (that's *two* years-in-a-row) Ash finished runner-up in the Women's

Singles at the Sydney International, which means she finished *second* (that's position Number *two*.) She was beaten by *two*-time Wimbledon winner and former World Number *Two*, Petra Kvitova from the Czech Republic. Then, in a Quarter Final at the Australian Open Petra beat Ash again. (Do the maths – that's *two* times!)

(Can you now see how "*two* many times" kinda, sorta, maybe works?)

But there was no three-peat!

The next time they played, Ash beat Petra in a Quarter Final of the Miami Open, in the USA. That year the prestigious tournament boasted its largest purse of prizemoney in its thirty-five year-history.

Ash went on to win it, the biggest victory to that point of her career. She collected $1.3 million US dollars (which is more than $1.8 million Australian dollars!)

But money does not buy success. Ash had earned hers through the combination of hard work and her rare gift to play brilliant tennis.

It was this combination that steered her towards Paris, one of the world's most romantic cities. The Seine River, cobblestones, sidewalk cafes, the buttery warmth of freshly made croissants...mmmm, yum! And then there is the French language that flows gloriously off the tongue:

Paris ne s'est pas fait en un jour!

(Translation: Paris wasn't built in a day.)

Indeed, it wasn't. The origins of the city date back more than 2000 years, and the city's old-world charm is one reason why Paris is referred to as the "City of Love."

And that brings us back to tennis.

Have you ever wondered how the term **LOVE** became used in the sport?

Remember, **LOVE** in tennis means **ZERO**.

Some people believe that someone once said that they played for the love of the game, meaning they enjoyed tennis so much that there was no need for incentives such as money or trophies. In other words, they were happy to play for nothing, zero, nought, 0.

Another theory is that **LOVE** is like the French word ***L'oeuf*** which means ***the egg*** and because the number zero (0) looks like an egg, at some point in tennis history, l'oeuf was used to describe zero (0), and it is now the accepted term.

(It's at this point that you may wish to accept a little bit of advice. That is, be careful when contemplating your first meal for the day. If you don't want eggs for breakfast, would you say: Love l'oeufs? Or does that mean you love eggs, and you in fact want a lot for breakfast? Confusing, huh?)

Regardless of theories, there was no doubting Ash **LOVED** playing tennis when, in late May, she strode onto the red clay – ***terra battue*** – courts at a Paris venue which was named in memory of the famous French aviator and World War One fighter pilot, Roland Garros.

The 2019 Internationaux de France de Tennis (the French Open) was underway.

DASH. DART. DELIGHT!

Ash won her Round One match against American, Jessica Pegula.

Now here's something unusual: Jessica's billionaire parents own the Buffalo Bills NFL team. That's American football. You know, the football played with helmets. It has the Superbowl, cheerleaders, thirty-cm-long hotdogs, and crazy, crazy fans who get together in stadium carparks before games and roar themselves silly. Let's Go Buffalo!

And...

IMMERSE. IGNITE. INSPIRE!

Ash won her Round Two match against another American, Danielle Collins. (You might remember that name? Go back to the first chapter, if you like.)

THREATEN. THRILL. THRIVE!

Ash won her Round Three match against German, Andrea Petkovic, in just sixty minutes.

SERVE. SLICE. SIZZLE!

Ash won her Round Four match against yet another American, Sofia Kenin. (Rod Rocket Laver was watching in the crowd. Fifty years earlier he'd won the French Open. Was this a good omen?)

RALLY. RESIST. REJOICE!

Ash won her Quarter Final against, would-you-believe-it, yes, an American, Madison Keys.

Let's add **REVENGE** here because at the 2017 French Open Madison had beaten Ash in the first round.

EXCITE. ENERGISE. ERUPT!

The semi-final… hang on, we might change things a little here.

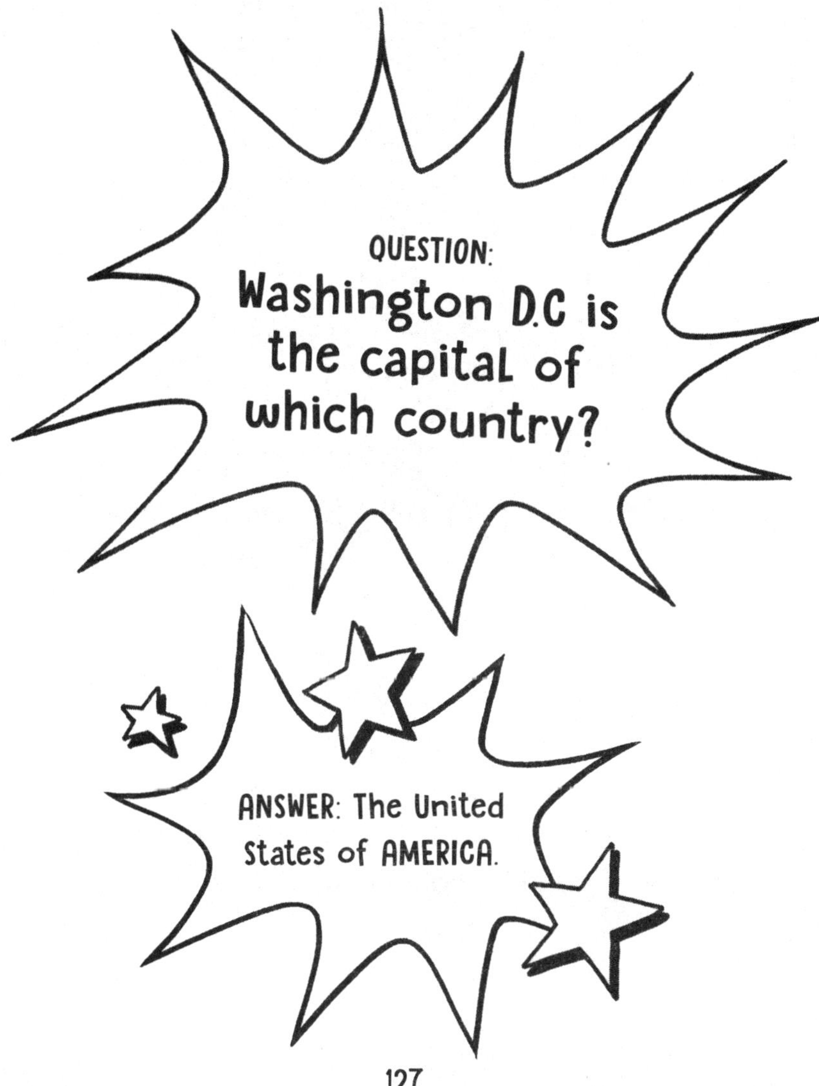

You know where this is going, don't you? Ash won her Semi Final against Amanda Anisimova who just happens to be, yep, an American.

So, after beating **FIVE** US players (and a German player) it was on to the decider. Twenty-three-year-old Ashleigh Barty against nineteen-year-old Marketa Vondrousova from the Czech Republic, both in their first Singles Final at a Grand Slam event. Ash, the tournament's Number Eight seed, was the favourite to win. But favouritism brings pressure. How would Ash handle it?

At least part of the answer can be found in what Ash told the media after her Semi Final win against Amanda Anisimova:

> It's an amazing opportunity for myself and my team. We have worked so hard to put ourselves in these positions. Now, we get to go out there and really enjoy it... That's the only way to approach it is to go out and enjoy it, have fun, try and play with freedom. That's ultimately when I play my best tennis and that's what we are after.

Did you notice some special words in Ash's statement?

Fun. (Back to FUNdamentals we go!)

Freedom.

Enjoy.

Any others? How about two words that were (and still are!) so very important to Ash:

Team and ***We.***

In singles tennis a player can often feel very much like they are doing it all on their own, but Ash did not think that way. She was all about working together with those around her, and while she was the only one on court, she knew she had so many people who'd helped her get there. And every one of them was on her side.

Ash was part of a team.

We.

Friends and family, supporters, and the special group that helped her prepare day-in, day-out. Her trainer, manager, physiotherapist, and her coach, Craig Tyzzer, a former professional player who'd been with Ash since she'd returned from her hiatus. Craig was the dad of four children. He understood Ash, and they worked brilliantly together. There was also, Ben Crowe, a mindset coach who helped Ash best prepare mentally for matches and think positively and confidently when playing.

On 8 June 2019, the results of all that work showed at Roland Garros when Ash blasted past Marketa Vondrousova to win **6-1**, **6-3**.

In the moments after the match, Ash put her hands to her head, she hugged her opponent across the net, she shook the chair umpire's hand, then she applauded the 15,000 strong crowd as though she was saying...

THANK YOU FOR BEING PART OF THIS MAGICAL DAY!

Ash had become the first Australian woman to win the French Open Singles since Margaret Court achieved the honour in 1973.

Two weeks later, Ash won the *Birmingham Classic* in England.

It was played on grass, meaning Ash had now won tournaments on hard court, clay, and grass all in the one year.

If those achievements weren't enough to have her jumping, there was another scintillating achievement: Ash had risen to Number One in the WTA world rankings. Only one other Australian woman had ever achieved the feat.

Who do you think it was?

Yet again, Ash's achievements had become part of a story that was much bigger than sport: Ash and Evonne, two Indigenous Australians who'd climbed to the top of the world.

BRILLIANT!

But how many more similarities could they share? This would be one time when we could say too many times would never be enough.

CHAPTER EIGHT

UPS AND DOWNS, UPS AND...

Media conferences are a key part of elite sport. In tennis, they generally go something like this...

A player sits behind a table in a room. The table is littered with microphones, mini recorders, and phones.

Journalists, often with notepads, sit or stand and ask the player questions.

The questions can go on for ages, and whatever the player says may be repeated in news bulletins and articles, and on social media platforms across the world. These answers are known as quotes, sound-bites or grabs.

Yeh, I was happy.
I'm really confident, but I won't be taking the game lightly.
I'm really excited to be here.
I was thinking only about the next point.
It was no use getting worked up over the mistake I'd made.

These conferences can be predictable, with journalists asking the same questions and players giving the same answers. Yet the conferences can also be intimidating, especially for young players who are not used to being in the spotlight.

Thankfully, Ash was now so familiar with the atmosphere that she felt comfortable enough to have some fun at her conferences during Wimbledon 2019.

Do any of those lines sound familiar? That's right, these are references to Disney movies! The Lion King, The Little Mermaid and Toy Story.

Because where would an elite tennis player be if she couldn't be inspired by the mighty Buzz Lightyear?

Ash was certainly in a relaxed mood and showed no signs of worrying about the weight of public expectation back home in Australia. She was the top seed at Wimbledon, and the World's Number One, which meant she was a target for every other player to try to knock down.

But that would not change anything in Ash's approach.

Ash just went about doing what she did, which included kicking a football that she always took on tour with her.

Also, just days before Wimbledon began, she visited Lords Cricket Ground to watch Australia beat England in a preliminary match of the Men's One Day International (ODI) World Cup. After the match, Ash met the Aussie players in the dressing room.

England won the ODI later that year, knocking Australia out in a Semi Final and then beating New Zealand in a nail-biting Final. It wasn't all defeat for the Aussies though, Australia defeated England in the multi-format Women's Ashes!

There were so many amazing sporting events in Europe in summer – the Women's World Cup in Football (soccer), the Tour de France in cycling, the British Open golf tournaments and the British Grand Prix – but for Ash, it was all about tennis!

Her first three rounds at Wimbledon went according to the hopes of Team Barty. Three wins, all in straight sets.

Then, the fourth match looked as though it was heading the same way. In her opening game against American Alison Riske, Ash served four missiles.

BOOM!

BOOM!

BOOM!

BOOM!

Four aces. Game over.

And the first set soon was too.

(If we're talking missiles, perhaps Alison Riske knows more about them than most tennis players because her father is an ex-operative of the US Secret Service and FBI!)

Anyway. Alison Launched OPERATION COMEBACK and she beat Ash.

3–6

6–2

6–3.

It's natural that disappointment can follow defeat, but in her media conference after her loss, Ash said something that should be bottled-up and preserved for all of us:

> Today wasn't my day. You know, I didn't win a tennis match; it's not the end of the world. It's a game. I love playing the game. I do everything in my power to try and win every single tennis match but that's not the case. So, I think today, it's disappointing right now, but give me an hour or so we'll be all good. You know, the sun's still going to come up tomorrow.

Then Ash smiled. And some hardened journalists in the room did too.

The sun continued to do its usual day-in-day-out-thing, and as it did, Ash bounced back from her Wimbledon exit to cast a shadow over her rivals. In the topsy-turvy world of rankings, she lost her Number One status for four weeks to Japan's Naomi Osaka, but by the end of 2019 there was no question Ash was atop the summit.

Or perhaps it's better said that Ash finished poll position on the grid because her prize for being the most successful women's singles player of the year was...

Brrrrrrrrrrrrrrrrrrrrrm!

A PORSCHE!

She received it before playing her final tournament for 2019, in Shenzhen, China. It was the WTA championship which was a shoot-out between the year's eight most successful players.

Ash made it all the way to the Final where she took on defending champion and World Number Eight, Elina Svitolina from Ukraine. History was on the side of Svitolina who had won her five previous matches against Ash. But history isn't only to be read about; it can be created as well, and in a match lasting one-and-a-half hours – a mere blink in the life of the universe – Ash carved her own space on the timeline.

She won **6-4 6-3** in an awesome display that fittingly justified her position in the sport.

Yet again, her name was mentioned in the same breath as Evonne Goolagong Cawley who won the title in 1974 and 1976, and finished runner-up in 1978.

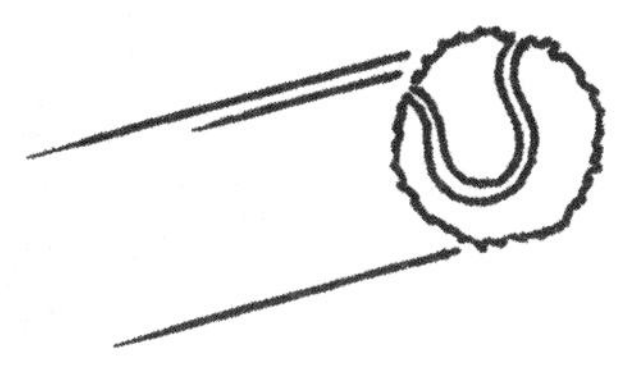

The win also gave Ash some petrol money to use in her new porsche – ***the winner's cheque was the biggest ever in women's and men's professional tennis – approximately $6.5 million Australian dollars!***

CHEQUE TO : Ash Barty No. 649

PAY TO THE ORDER OF:

$6.5 million dollars

Treasurer, WTA

It can be easy to get lost in the seas of numbers and glitz of the highest profile events, but Ash also achieved another honour that underlined her devotion, not only to tennis, but Australia and her fellow-players.

She became the first Australian to be awarded the International Tennis Federation's *Fed Cup Heart Award* for her performances and commitment to her team, country, and competition. As part of the prize, she was given

$14,000 to donate to a charity. She chose the RSPCA. Since her childhood, cats and dogs had been part of her life, and she yearned to help all animals.

The year was 2019.

The champion, both on court and off court, was Ash Barty.

CHAPTER NINE

FAMILY. ABOVE ALL, FAMILY

A year later, another media conference. But this time there's not a Buzz Lightyear in sight; instead, there's a bit of drool and Goo-Goo-Gaa-Gaa.

You see, after losing a Semi Final at the 2020 Australian Open, Ash sat down at her conference nursing a baby girl on her lap. Again, after the disappointment of a loss, she made the room smile.

This is my newest niece. My sister had her, what, eleven, twelve weeks ago – yeh, this is what life's all about. It's amazing.

A few minutes later, after a few little cries from baby Olivia, Ash gently bounced her niece, and said:

Life is a beautiful thing. She brought a smile to my face as soon as I came off the court. I get to give her a hug, and it's all good, it's all good.

Unfortunately, 2020 was not the year of hugs.

In fact, we all know it was the year of social distancing. Covid-19 was changing the world. Tennis changed too. For the first time since World War II, Wimbledon was cancelled, and although the US and French Opens were held, Ash did not compete in them. Instead, she chose to stay in Australia for much of the year.

She played just four tennis tournaments in 2020 but being at home gave her the opportunity to participate in another competition: she won the Women's Championship at her local golf club, Brookwater, where her boyfriend, Garry Kissick, was working as a trainee professional.

From tennis to cricket to golf, Ash could watch a ball closely and give it a mighty WHACK!

By then, Ash had also been named the 2020 Young Australian of the Year. In accepting the award from former World Number One, Pat Rafter, who surprised her with it during the Australian Open that year, Ash shone the light on the two most influential people in her life.

All of my values that I live by, that I try and live by every single day, regardless of whether it's in sport or in life, all come from mum and dad. It's about being humble, being respectful, and then just giving it a crack, just being the best that you can be, and that's all you can ask of yourself.

By 2021, Australia was also asking questions of Ash as another Open took place at Melbourne Park. Again, Ash moved through the early rounds but lost in a Quarter Final.

So be it. Move on. What's next?

After winning two Singles titles (Miami and Stuttgart, Germany) and finishing runner-up in another (Madrid, Spain), Ash suffered a hip injury and withdrew during the second round of the French Open.

So be it. Move on. What's next?

Wimbledon.

Remember?

Wimbledon.

Courts of brilliant green lawn mown in exquisite strips.

WIMBLEDON.

Strawberries and cream.

WIMBLEDON.

Royalty and movie stars.

WIMBLEDON!

Can you also remember when Ash won the Junior Girl's Singles title at this most illustrious of sporting venues?

That's right. Back in 2011, when Ash was fifteen years old.

She was now twenty-five, an amazingly successful young woman who'd stepped on and off a rollercoaster – and a merry-go-round and a rocket – for so much of her life!

Her journey still promised so many enticing destinations, and her return to Wimbledon offered a symbolic landing point. Fifty years earlier, Evonne Goolagong Cawley had won the first of her two Singles crowns at Wimbledon. If Ash was to follow in the steps of her great mentor and friend, ***she would have to play at her awesome best.***

DASH. DART. DELIGHT. WIN.

IMMERSE. IGNITE. INSPIRE. WIN.

THREATEN. THRILL. THRIVE. WIN.

SERVE. SLICE. SIZZLE. WIN.

RALLY. RESIST. REJOICE. WIN.

EXCITE. ENERGISE. ERUPT. WIN.

She did all of that and then, there were only two players left:

Ash Barty
AUS
KaroLina PLiskova
CZ

- **Australia vs Czech Republic**
- **Twenty-five years old vs Twenty-nine years old**
- **1.66 metres vs 1.86 metres**
- **Top Seed vs Number Eight Seed**
- **Winner of One Major Singles Final vs Runner-Up in One Major Singles Final.**

Imagine how nerve-wracking it would be to step out on to centre court...

Fingers trembling, voice quivering, legs shaking kind of nervous, like when you do a speech in front of the whole class, or worse still, the whole school. It can feel like you are a tiny ant looking up an elephant's foot that's about to squash you.

Now, imagine this, while you are feeling that nervous you must hit a tennis ball with a racquet.

Back and forth, back and forth, back and forth.

Your every shot, ***your every mistake***, is watched by a crowd of nearly 15,000 people.

They ***Oooh*** and they ***Aaah!***

Also, there are tens of millions of others watching on screens across the world as you try to win a trophy that you've dreamed of holding since you first swung a racquet as a child.

Down comes the elephant's foot.

Well, that's how *Karolina* kind of felt when the Final began.

Ash, though, looked cool and calm, and she won the first fourteen points.

Click your finger, just like that.

POINT. POINT. POINT. POINT. POINT. POINT. POINT. POINT. POINT. POINT. POINT. POINT. POINT. POINT.

Ash won the first set, **6–3**.

But that ant was doing everything to dodge the elephant's foot!

Karolina grew in confidence.

The second set was a thriller that went to a tiebreaker.

Karolina won. Sets level.

For all the Ash Barty fans cheering across the planet, a key moment came early in the deciding set when Ash broke Karolina's serve in only the second game.

Karolina tried and tried to fight back. She gave everything she had. But Ash was in control. This was her day.

The final score was...

6–3

6–7

6–3

...in nearly two hours of captivating sporting theatre.

After she won, Ash dropped to her haunches and cried. And, no doubt, many people back in Australia shed tears as well.

Of the many words she said in interviews afterwards, there were six simple ones that showed how much winning Wimbledon meant to her:

I hope I made Evonne proud.

You did, Ash. You defo did!

It was forty-one years since an Australian woman – Evonne in 1980 – had won the Singles title at Wimbledon.

Wimbledon!

One of the world's most prestigious sports events.

WIMBLEDON!

The history, the traditions, the fame.

WIMBLEDON!

Names and deeds that last forever.

WIMBLEDON!

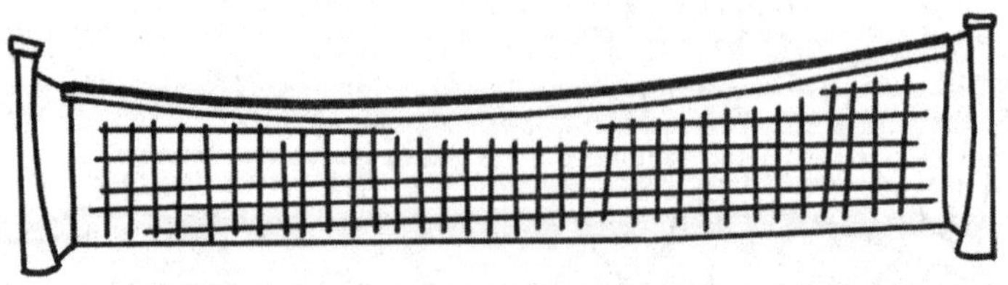

But a month later, the unpredictable beauty of tennis played its hand and Ash lost in the first round of Singles at the *Tokyo 2020 Olympics*.

Hang on a minute, aren't we talking about 2021? Well, yes. But because of Covid, the Olympic Games were postponed until 2021. The organisers decided to keep 2020 in the official title. Maybe they had already printed all the signs and banners? Maybe that's another Kahoot topic for you?

Or perhaps you could ask:

Ash finished the year as she'd started it. She was Number One in WTA Singles rankings.

(And in the years ahead, a certain person named Olivia would have lots to tell others about her amazing Aunty Ash!)

CHAPTER TEN
WHO IS ASH BARTY?

So, now we come back to where this book began. The evening of Saturday, January 29th, 2022 at the Australian Open, the Rod Laver Arena, at a buoyant Melbourne Park.

Ash had just beaten American Danielle Collins to win her third Grand Slam Singles title. In lounge rooms across Australia fists were pumped, drinks were spilt, and adults mixed sternness with happiness to tell children:

All right, you can stay up a bit longer, but you MUST go to bed after the presentation.

Ash stood on court waiting to receive a shining piece of silverware that is named in honour of one of Australia's greatest tennis players. Nearly one hundred years ago, between 1924 and 1931, Daphne Akhurst dominated women's tennis in this country, winning five Australian Singles and nine Doubles titles.

The Daphne Akhurst Memorial Cup, presented to the Women's Singles Champion, is a perpetual trophy, which means it is presented every time the Australian Open is staged. The champion doesn't get to keep the trophy, but their name is engraved on it to keep company with the other winners and the champion is given a replica trophy instead.

Suddenly, in a moment that surprised everyone except the organisers, one of those names was announced to the crowd...

And then Evonne Goolagong Cawley emerged from the darkness and waved to the delighted fans. She was the most special of guests who'd been invited to present the champion's cup.

Ash smiled, her eyes sparkling brighter than the trophy. The two legends hugged, then Evonne stepped back as Ash stood in front of the microphone. She thanked her family, her team, the organisers, the crowd, and then she finished with words that lit up *Rod Laver Arena*:

This is just a dream come true for me, and I'm so proud to be an Aussie. So, thank you so much everyone. We'll see you next time.

Ash gave a quick thumbs up, and when she caught the eyes of Evonne, she saw a double-thumbs up being sent back her way. It was one of many feel-good moments on a priceless night.

Four weeks later, Ash stood with her champion's trophy in front of one of the world's most breath-taking, spiritual, and meaningful landmarks: Uluru. Shining silverware, red-dust, and a young Indigenous Australian **connecting to the heartbeat of our nation**.

It was Ash's first trip to this sacred place.

She was there in her role as the Indigenous Ambassador for Tennis Australia, participating in the *Racquets and Red Dust* program.

After erecting a makeshift net in the bush, she played tennis with children from the *Mutitjulu* school, which is part of a small community inside Uluru-Kata National Park.

She did the same with young people in Alice Springs. These were not only the most golden of golden moments for the children, but also for Ash who continues to learn about her heritage and what it means. The lessons will continue for all of us.

For Ash, the classroom has been the world. Uluru, Paris, Miami, Shenzhen, Cincinnati, Toronto, Birmingham, Rome, Madrid. And wherever she has gone she has upheld the values of good sportsmanship and fair play.

The tennis experts and the fans expected Ash to continue her incredible journey, but in March 2022, she announced her retirement from playing professional tennis. She was one month short of turning twenty-six years old. It was time for new chapters in her life...

Chapters yet to be written.

Thank you, Ash, for all you have given us. And good luck for today, tomorrow, and every day after that. May they be full of joy.

Well played, Ash.

CHAPTER ELEVEN
THAT'S IT
(FOR THE MOMENT)

So, what do you think?

How **DID** Ash get so good? What would it take to be a professional tennis player?

Or maybe ask yourself a different question:

How can YOU BE THE VERY BEST THAT YOU CAN BE when you play any sport?

Here are some suggestions to get you started:

☆ HAVE FUN! AND LOVE WHAT YOU DO!

That doesn't mean you have to enjoy every single millisecond of playing and training. That would be impossible, wouldn't it? Let's get real here!

Yes, there will be times when you don't enjoy what's happening. Like, when the sun is glaring at you, and your eyes are stinging with sweat and you just can't stop your feet from feeling as though they've been hit by a sledgehammer and you're losing **BIG TIME** and all the cheering from the spectators seems to come for your opponent, and there isn't a blade of grass or a speck of *terra battue* that you can hide under.

You can sometimes feel all... alone.

Nah, that might not be fun. But that's tennis. That's sport. That's life. It can happen.

However, one of the most powerful things about sport is that **YOU CAN GET LOST IN THE**

MOMENT, and you can be so focused on that moment that nothing else matters... not your maths exam next Monday, not the barbeque you have to go to where there'll be no-one your age to play with, not the fact that your skateboard is broken...

Getting lost in the moment can be the most magical place for anyone to be!

Getting lost in the moment is **FUN!** So is winning. And being with friends.

And shadow-hitting down the corridor outside your bedroom on game day!

And blasting a good shot!

And chasing a ball from side to side only to lose the point and the match yet you still manage to smile because you loved doing it...

FUN, FUN, FUN, FUN, FUN, FUN, FUN!

Why not write your own list about why playing tennis or any sport is fun for you?

☆ TRAIN LIKE YOU MEAN IT!

First of all, that means **FITNESS**.

Oh no, not another one of those tests...

BEEP!

Run twenty metres. Cross the line. Turnaround.

BEEP!

Run twenty metres. Cross the line. Turnaround.

BEEP!

Run twenty metres. Cross the line. Turnaround.

BEEP!

Scamper twenty metres. Cross the line. Turnaround.

BEEP!

Scamper twenty metres, Cross the line, Turnaround.

PUFF! BEEP!

Sprinttwentymetrescrossthelineturnaround.

BEEP!

Sprinttwentymetrescrossthelineturnaround.

BEEP!

Sprinttwentymetrescrossthelineturnaround.

BEEP!

Sprinttwentymetrescrossthelineturnaround.

BEE–EEEEP!

WHEW!

Ouch!

Just think of all the fitness work that Ash put in over many years.

Ash was super fit. And that fitness helped her play tennis as best she could. And that fitness also helped her when she was **PRACTISING HER TECHNIQUE**. Which she also did **A LOT**.

Also, the practice helped her fitness. So, one helped the other. The simple message here is:

Ash Barty trained hard.

MAKE THE MOST OF YOUR ABILITIES (whatever they are)

The truth of life is that we all have different abilities, and we use them in different ways. Of course, not everyone can serve at 180 kilometres an hour, or be so accurate that they can land a shot on a coin from the other side of the court. That means we can't all be as successful as Ash was in tennis.

(Remember those hundreds-and-thousands?)

However, it is always rewarding to make the most of your abilities. **To be the very best that you can be.** That's cool. So, how do you achieve that?

Well, you can start by having fun and training, but there is a really, really important point that deserves its own heading...

TRY YOUR HARDEST

It's as simple as that. Ash didn't always win, but she always tried, tried, and tried. And then she tried some more. That determination and willingness earned her respect all over the world.

That is how you win, even when you lose.

TRY TO KEEP YOUR HEAD IN THE GAME

By this I mean, *think* about the way you *think* – there's a fancy word for this called **MINDSET** and it can cover a lot of things, which all helped Ash along her way to No. 1.

Being POSITIVE.

Being RESILIENT.

ACCEPTING CHALLENGES.

LEARNING from DEFEAT.

LEARNING from WINNING.

UNDERSTANDING YOURSELF.

HAPPINESS.

SELF BELIEF.

That's quite a long list, but you could come up with your own words that help make up your attitudes to how you play your sport. (And also live your life!)

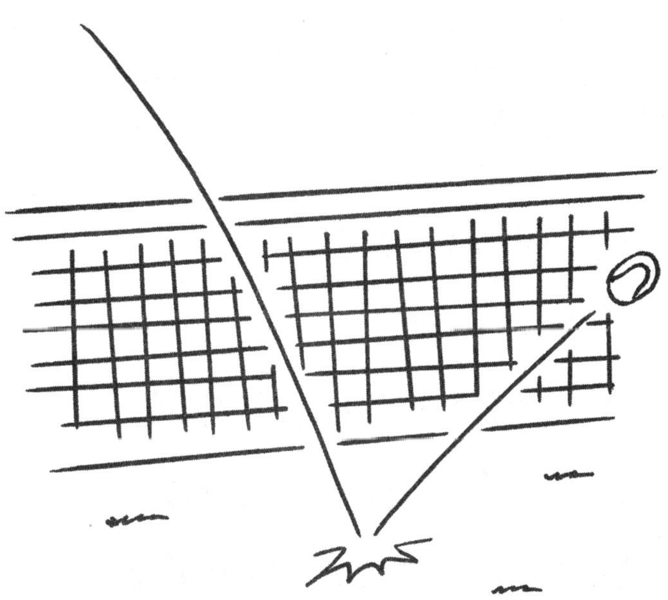

THERE'S NO "I" IN TEAM

You might think that is a pretty cheesy saying (and I'm sure you've heard it before), but it's still used because it is so relevant to us all. Ash lived by it, and she continues to recognise that so many people have been part of her journey.

So, time for another question for you. Who is part of your team? Friends? Family? Coaches? Mentors? The bus-driver who gets you to your matches on time? The local café owner who sponsors your club? The mums and dads who run the barbeque every Saturday morning? Tennis and all sports are about community. People helping one another. It makes us feel good.

Yep, there's no "I" in TEAM.

So, what are we missing on this list? How about a word that sneaked in a couple of points earlier:

What does it mean to you? Do you respect your teammates? Do you respect the opposition? Do you respect yourself? Do you respect the sport you play?

Ash did. All the time.

That's yet another reason why we respect her so very much.

And what about another word that definitely applies to Ash.

What a powerful word. Ash was unbelievable at playing tennis. But she didn't need to boast about her brilliance. Her performances spoke for her.

Humility means that no matter how great you are at what you do – ***even as great as being Number One tennis player in the whole world*** – you realise that you are no more important than anyone else.

So, there you have it. All you have read in this chapter is just a starting list for you because only ***YOU*** are ***YOU***, and it is up to ***YOU*** to determine how you play your sport, and what you do in life.

It's the same for Ash. ***What will she do next?***

There's no doubt we will find out more about Ash in the years to come. Until then...

K-toink-whack

K-toink-whack

K-toink-whack

K-toink-whack

K-toink-whack

K-toink-whack...

Keep going. You never know what might happen.

Name: Ashleigh Barty

Born: 24 April 1996

Career High Ranking: Number One

Grand Slam Event Singles Championships: 3 (French Open, 2019; Wimbledon 2021; Australian Open 2022)

Grand Slam Event Doubles Championships: 1 (US Open, 2018)

WTA Singles Record: 305 wins/102 losses

Career Prize Money: $US 23,829,071

Olympic Medals: 1 Bronze, Mixed Doubles (Tokyo 2020… but remember it was held in 2021)

Awards include:

- US Open Sportsmanship Award (2021 & 2018)
- WTA Player of the Year (2021 & 2019)
- Newcombe Medal (2021, 2019, 2018, 2017)
- Young Australian of the Year (2020)
- Fed Cup Heart Award (2019)
- Sport Australia Hall of Fame 'Don Award' (2019)
- National Dreamtime Awards: Female Sportsperson of the Year (2019-2018-2017)
- AIS Sports Awards: Sports Personality of the Year (2019), Female Athlete of the Year (2019), Sporting Moment of the Year (2019).

April 1996: Born in Ipswich, Queensland

2001: Starts training with Jim Joyce at West Brisbane Tennis centre

2008: Wins Under 12 Australian Girls' Singles Hardcourt Championship at Melbourne Park.

2009: When just thirteen years old, she plays junior tournaments in Europe and New Zealand.

2010: Plays her first professional tournament in her hometown, Ipswich, and she also attends an Adidas Development Camp in Las Vegas where she meets Steffi Graf and Andre Agassi.

2011: Wins Junior Girls Singles Wimbledon title. In this year Ash played all four Junior Major tournaments. Also plays for Australia in the Junior Fed Cup, and finishes the year ranked Number Two Junior Girl tennis player in the world.

January 2012: At fifteen years of age, she makes her debut at the Australian Open, and loses in the first round. Later in the year she also plays at the French Open and Wimbledon.

2013: Partners with fellow Australian Casey Dellacqua to win the Birmingham Women's Doubles title. They also were runners-up at the Australian Open and Wimbledon.

2014: At eighteen years of age Ash decides to stop playing professional tennis. Returns to help her very first coach, Jim Joyce, coach players of all ages.

2015–early 2016: Plays as a batting all-rounder for the Western Suburbs District Cricket Club in the Queensland Women's Premier Grade competition. Gets picked for the Brisbane Heat and plays the initial season of Australia's WBBL (Women's Big Bash League).

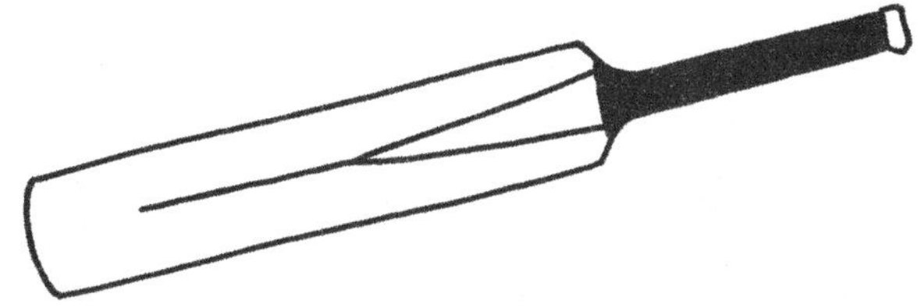

2016: Returns to playing professional tennis.

2017: Wins her first WTA Women's Singles Title, the Malaysian Open in Kuala Lumpur.

2018: Partners American Coco Vandeweghe to win the Women's Doubles Title at the US Open.

2019: Wins the Women's Singles at the Miami Open and claims $1.8 million (Aus), the biggest win to that point of her career. Then wins the French Open, her first Major Singles title. Also moves to World Number One and completes the year by winning the WTA Championship in China. She takes home a record $6.5 for the victory.

2020: Named Young Australian of the Year. Also, the Covid epidemic affects the scheduling of world tennis events. Wimbledon is cancelled. Ash chooses to spend much of the year in Australia. Plays some golf and wins the Women's Championship at her local club, Brookwater.

2021: Wins the Women's Singles crown at Wimbledon.

January 2022: Wins the Women's Singles Final at the Australian Open, defeating American Danielle Collins.

March 2022: Retires from playing professional tennis.

GLOSSARY OF PEOPLE

Andre Agassi: American tennis great from the 1980s, 1990s and early 2000s who won eight Major singles titles and an Olympic gold medal.

Daphne Akhurst (1903–1933): Five-time winner of the Australian Women's Singles Championship between 1925 and 1930. The Australian Open Women's Singles trophy is named in her honour.

Amanda Anisimova: Current American tennis player, born in 2001 who has risen to a career-high World ranking of 21.

Pierre Babolat: The inventor of natural gut tennis strings, who lived in Lyon, France. His company, *Babolat and Monnier,* processed natural gut for a variety of products including sausages and music strings. In 1875 they experimented using the gut for tennis strings, and the rest is, as they say, history.

Reginald Leslie "Snowy" Baker (1884–1953): Multi-talented Australian athlete of the early 1900s, who represented Australia in swimming, diving, and boxing at the London Olympics of 1908.

Usain Bolt: Eight-time Olympic gold medallist sprinter from Jamaica, who holds the world records for the 100m sprint at 9.58 seconds, and the 200m at 19.19 seconds. He is one of the greatest athletes of all time.

Donald Bradman: Australia's most famous ever cricketer who finished his career with a test batting average of 99.94. He played from the 1920s to 1940s and is revered as a national hero by Australians.

Henry Bruce (1884–1958): A former Queensland politician. A national schools tennis tournament is named after him.

Darren Cahill: Former Australian professional tennis player, and elite coach who played during the 1980s and 90s. The players he has coached include Lleyton Hewitt, Andre Agassi, and Simona Halep.

Jennifer Capriati: America's former World Number One, and winner of three Major Singles titles and an Olympic Gold medal 1992. She made her professional debut when just thirteen.

Kim Clijsters: Former Belgian tennis player and the winner of four Major singles titles between 2005 and 2011.

Evonne Goolagong Cawley: One of Australia's all-time favourite athletes. A *Wiradjuri* woman who won seven Major Singles titles and was a World Number One. She is a mentor of Ash Barty.

Danielle Collins: Current American tennis player and runner-up to Ash Barty at the 2022 Australian Open.

Trent Cotchin: An AFL (Australian Football League) player for the Richmond Tigers and captain of the winning club in 2017, 2019, and 2020.

Margaret Court: Australian tennis great who still holds the record for women and men as the winner of twenty-four Major Singles titles, and sixty-four Major titles (Singles, Women's Doubles, Mixed Doubles).

Ben Crowe: Ash Barty's mindset coach, who is known for instilling positive attitudes into players. He has worked with such athletes and teams as Ash, Dylan Alcott and the Richmond Tigers.

Russel Crowe: New Zealand movie-star and sports fan.

Casey Dellacqua: Former Australian professional tennis player who retired in 2018. Doubles partner and close friend of Ash.

Novak Djokovic: One of the all-time greats of Men's tennis. The Serbian superstar has won twenty Major Singles titles.

Roger Federer: The Swiss machine! Another all-time great, and winner of twenty Major Singles titles.

Cathy Freeman: Two- time World Champion and winner of Sydney 2000 Olympic Games Gold in the 400metres. An Australian legend of the *Birri Gubba* people, who will always be remembered for proudly carrying the Aboriginal flag onto the track.

RoLand Garros: Home of the French Open, in Paris. The complex, which was built in 1928, has twenty courts. It is named after a French war hero and aviator who was killed in World War I.

Cori "Coco" Gauff: Young American tennis player, who was born in 2004 and is tipped to be a superstar in the making.

Steffi Graf: There have been few better tennis players in any era. A former World Number One for a record 377 weeks. The German won twenty-two Major Singles titles.

Lucie Hradecka: Current Women's tennis player from the Czech Republic, who has won two Major Women's doubles titles and a Mixed Doubles title.

John Howard: Former Australian Prime Minister, who held office between 1996 and 2007.

Jim Joyce: Ash Barty's junior tennis coach, who began coaching Ash when she was four years old. Later, when Ash took a break from tennis, she helped Jim coach people of all ages.

Sofia Kenin: Current American professional tennis player, and winner of the 2020 Women's Singles at the Australian Open. Born in Russia in 1998 she and her family moved to the USA when she was just a baby. She soon became known as a child prodigy in tennis.

Madison Keys: Current American professional tennis player whose career-high singles ranking has been World Number Seven. She was runner-up in the 2017 Women's Singles at the US Open.

Irina Kromacheva: Current Russian professional tennis player with a career-high singles ranking of 89.

Petra Kvitova: Current professional tennis player from the Czech Republic, and winner of the Women's Singles titles at Wimbledon in 2011 and 2014.

Meg Lanning: Australian women's cricket captain from 2014 to the present. A record-breaking top-order batter, she has been a member of four of Australia's winning World Cup One Day International teams and has also been part of two T20 World Cup victories. She recently led Australia to a gold medal at the Commonwealth Games.

Rod Laver: The "Rockhampton Rocket". Winner of eleven Major Singles titles between 1960 and 1969, and the only player ever to win two Grand Slams (all four Majors in the same calendar year).

Dustin Martin: Richmond AFL player, who was part of the winning squad in 2017, 2019 and 2020.

Billy Moore: Former Queensland and Australian rugby league player who played in the 1980s and 90s. A rugged forward for the North Sydney Bears, he was known for his commitment and passion.

Rafael Nadal: With Federer and Djokovic, this Spanish phenomenon has been the star of a golden era in Men's Tennis. He is the winner of twenty-two Major Singles titles including fourteen at the French Open.

Chris O'Neill: Former Australian tennis player who won the Women's Singles at the 1978 Australian Open.

Naomi Osaka: Current Japanese professional tennis player and winner of four Major Singles titles.

John Peers: Current Australian professional tennis player who specialises in Doubles and partnered with Ash to win the Mixed Doubles bronze medal at the Tokyo 2020 Olympics.

Jessica Pegula: Current American professional tennis player with a career-high World Singles ranking of Number Seven. Reached the quarter-finals of the Australian Open in 2021 and 2022, and the 2022 French Open.

Andrea Petkovic: Current German professional tennis player whose career-high ranking is World Number Nine. She reached the Women's Singles semi-finals of the 2014 French Open.

Nova Peris: Aboriginal Australian and member of Australia's Gold medal winning Women's hockey team at the 1996 Atlanta Olympics. Switched to athletics and won Gold in the 200 metres and 4 x 100 m relay at the 1998 Commonwealth Games in Kuala Lumpur.

Ellyse Perry: Multi-talented athlete who has represented Australia in cricket and soccer, but from 2014 onwards she has concentrated solely on cricket. Considered one of the best all-rounders to have played women's cricket.

Karolina Pliskova: Current professional tennis player from the Czech Republic who was ranked Number One in the World for eight weeks in 2017.

Pat Rafter: Former Australian professional tennis player, and winner of the Men's Singles titles at US Open in 1997-1998. He played at the top level in the 1990's and early 2000's. Renowned for his likeable "boy next door" personality.

Nicole Richardson: Winner of Olympic Bronze with the Australian Women's softball team at the Atlanta Olympics in 1996 and winner of Gold with the Australian Netball team at the 2002 Commonwealth Games in Manchester.

Daniel Rioli: Richmond AFL footballer, who was part of the winning club in 2017, 2019 and 2020.

Alison Riske: Current American professional tennis player whose career-high Singles Ranking is Number Eighteen. Reached the Women's Singles quarter-finals of Wimbledon 2019.

Luke Saville: Current Australian professional men's tennis player who won the 2011 Junior Wimbledon crown in Boys' Singles, and the 2012 Junior Australian Open.

Maria Sharapova: Former Russian professional player, and winner of five Major Singles titles between 2006 and 2014.

Jason Stoltenberg: Former Australian tennis player who grew up in the small town of Narrabri, country New South Wales. He played at the elite level from the late 1980s to early 2000s. After retiring from playing, he turned to coaching.

Samantha Stosur: Current Australian professional tennis player and winner of the Women's Singles at 2011 US Open, and a four-time winner of Major Women's Double titles.

Elina Svitolina: Current Ukrainian professional tennis player, who has achieved a career-high Singles ranking of Number Three. Won the bronze medal in Women's Singles at Tokyo 2020.

Anna Tatishvili: Former Georgian-American professional tennis player who won eleven Singles and eight Doubles titles during her career. (Georgia is a country in Eastern Europe.)

Ian Thorpe: Nicknamed "the Thorpedo", he is one of Australia's swimming greats, winning five Olympic Gold medals, spanning the Sydney 2000 and Athens 2004 Games. Specialised in freestyle.

Craig Tyzzer: Tennis coach who linked up with Ash in 2016 and helped guide her to her three Major Singles titles.

Coco Vandeweghe: Current American professional tennis player who has ranked in the World's Top Ten. In 2017 she reached the Women's Singles semi-finals of the Australian Open and US Open.

Marketa Vondrousova: Current professional tennis player from the Czech Republic. Was just nineteen years old when she reached the Final of the Women's Singles French Open in 2019. She won silver in the Women's Singles at Tokyo 2020.

Serena Williams: One of the most famous athletes on the planet! Winner of twenty-three Major Singles titles between 1999 and 2017. Still playing tennis. Awesome!

Venus Williams: Nearly fifteen months older than her sister, Serena, and another superstar of the modern era, winning seven Major Singles titles, including Wimbledon five times.

GLOSSARY

Ace: A legal serve in tennis that the receiver can't hit. If you manage to serve up an ace then the point is yours!

All England Lawn Tennis and Croquet Club: Host of the Wimbledon tournament, which is held in the suburb of Wimbledon, on the outskirts of London, in June every year.

ATP: This stands for the Association of Tennis Professionals. It is the governing body that oversees the men's professional players and circuits.

Backhand: A shot in which the back of the hand faces the direction of the shot. A classic backhand is one-handed but it has become more common for players to hold the racquet with two hands, which can give the shot more power.

BBL: This stands for the Big Bash League, which is the annual national Men's T20 cricket tournament in Australia. It was established in 2011. The teams that play are: Perth Scorchers, Adelaide Strikers, Melbourne Renegades, Melbourne Stars, Hobart Hurricanes, Sydney Thunder, Sydney Sixers, and the Brisbane Heat.

Blues: The New South Wales rugby league team is known as the Blues and they wear a distinctive blue jumper.

Brisbane Heat: A team in the BBL and WBBL.

Bruce Cup: This is a national schools Twelve-and-under tennis competition which is held annually across Australia.

Davis Cup: International men's team tennis competition, which is held annually across the world and culminates in a Final between the two best teams.

FBI: This stands for the Federal Bureau of Investigation which is the US government organisation which investigates major crimes which threaten the national security of the United States. The FBI will be called in to take over investigations from state police when things get very serious.

Fed Cup: International women's team tennis competition, which is held annually in a similar way to the Davis Cup.

Forehand: the classic shot in tennis, played when the palm of the hand is facing in the direction of the stroke.

Grand Slam event: These are also known as the "Major" tournaments (see below) and they include the Australian Open, the French Open, Wimbledon and the US Open. Each of these events include a junior competition and a wheelchair tennis competition.

Grand Slam: If you win all our "Major" tournaments in the one calendar year it is called winning the Grand Slam

ITF: This stands for the International Tennis Federation, which is the body that oversees and regulates the rules of tennis and the international tournaments that take place each year.

Kahoot: This is a game-based learning platform, which is used in schools – with the aim of making lessons more exciting!

K-toink-whack: Make up your own definition!

Lob: A looping tennis shot that is hit high over the opponent's head so they have to run to try to hit it.

Love: This means zero in tennis. (Not to be confused with "l'oeuf", which means "the egg" in French. If you don't want eggs for breakfast, would you perhaps say "Love l'oeufs?" Or does that mean you love eggs, and you in fact want a lot for breakfast?)

Major: One of the four most prestigious tournaments in professional tennis – the Australian Open, the French Open, Wimbledon and the US Open. (also see *Grand Slam*)

Maroons: This is the nickname for the Queensland rugby league team and refers to the maroon jumpers worn by the team.

Melbourne Stars: This is a team in the BBL and WBBL competition. The players wear green uniforms but shouldn't be mistaken for the bright green ones worn by one of their opponents, the Sydney Thunder.

Men's One Day international (ODI) World Cup: This is a cricket competition in the fifty-overs-a-side format that takes place every four years and pits cricket teams from around the World in tournament that is usually hosted in one country. There is also a Women's ODI World Cup which takes place every four years.

Ngarigo: The Ngarigo people are indigenous Australians who come from the alpine regions of what is now New South Wales and Victoria.

RSPCA: The Royal Society for the Prevention of Cruelty to Animals is a charity founded nearly 200 years ago with the aim of protecting animals from ill treatment by humans.

Seed: This word is used to describe the rankings of the top players at a tennis tournament and originates from the idea of laying out or sowing seeds from smallest to largest in a garden bed.

Smash: A powerful shot in tennis, which is hit from above the player's head in a similar fashion to a serve.

Volley: A tennis shot where the racquet hits the ball on the full.

WBBL: Women's Big Bash League, the Women's national T20 competition in Australia. (see *BBL* above)

Wiradjuri: The Wiradjuri people are indigenous Australians whose roots are based in central New South Wales.

WTA: This stands for the Women's Tennis Association, which is the body which governs professional women's tennis across the world.